FINGER LAKES WINE
and the Legacy of
DR. KONSTANTIN FRANK

TOM RUSS

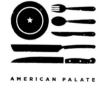

AMERICAN PALATE

Published by American Palate
A Division of The History Press
Charleston, SC 29403
www.historypress.net

Bottom front image and photo of grapes on back cover by Stu Gallagher,
permission of stugallagher.com.

Images used with the permission of Dr. Frank's Vinifera Wine Cellars
unless otherwise noted.

First published 2015

Manufactured in the United States

ISBN 978.1.62619.734.3

Library of Congress Control Number: 2014953438

For Karla, always.

CONTENTS

FOREWORD

K onstantin Frank is viewed as a true American patriot and pioneer. Born on July 4, 1899, in the Ukraine, he pioneered the introduction of the noble European grapes to the Finger Lakes and other eastern states. Konstantin wanted the eastern wine industry to prosper and was very giving with his knowledge and techniques to allow other vineyards and wineries to follow his lead. He felt that Americans deserved only the best wines produced from the *Vitis vinifera* wine grapes. At this time in the 1950s, the New York wine industry was in a state of "happy mediocrity." It was difficult for Konstantin to convince academia and other grape growers and wineries to switch to higher-quality *vinifera* when they were easily selling wines from native grapes that required less care.

Gradually, Americans began to demand higher-quality wines from the *vinifera* varieties such as Riesling, Chardonnay, Gewurztraminer, Pinot Noir and so on. This demand for better-quality wines was supplied quickly by California wineries, and the majority of New York wineries continued producing wines from the native *Vitis labrusca* grapes, resulting in lost market share. Several wineries even went out of business. Konstantin had a small group of "cooperators" who learned from and worked with him. Those "cooperators" later started wineries in other eastern states, leading to a renaissance in the wine quality of eastern wines. Today, all fifty states have wineries, and this has resulted in more Americans learning about wines and touring these regional wineries. This has created an increase in per capita wine consumption among Americans, and now the United States has become the largest wine market in the world.

The winery founded by Konstantin in 1962 is now in its fourth generation of family management. Dr. Frank's winery receives record numbers of gold medals in national and international wine competitions each year. Many of these awards are even higher in esteem than gold medals such as "Best of Class" or even "Sweepstakes Winner," chosen as best wine of the entire competition. In addition, there have been many accolades in the press praising Dr. Frank's wines and giving them high ratings. I welcome you to visit our beautiful winery overlooking Keuka Lake in Hammondsport for a tasting of these award-winning wines. In addition, please visit our website at www.drfrankwines.com to learn more about "New York's Most Award Winning Winery."

Our family is very grateful to Tom Russ for all of his time and dedicated research in writing this wonderful book. There have been several writers who started on similar projects but, for various reasons, did not follow through with their plans. I was getting discouraged that the wonderful story about Konstantin's life would never be told. In addition, I would like to thank all the family members and friends of Konstantin who spent many hours being interviewed by Tom and providing him with some great stories. Finally, I would like to thank Konstantin for being a loving grandfather and mentor to me.

I hope you enjoy the book as much as I have. Remember to always trust your convictions and never give up. Always carry on in what you believe in.

Cheers,
Frederick Frank

ACKNOWLEDGEMENTS

E very book requires the acknowledgement of people who have assisted the author in the effort to bring the book to life. Writing the story of a life—or, in this case, the story of a family—is not possible without help from many sources. The challenge of acknowledging those who have helped is trying to include everyone.

The staff at the New York State Agricultural Experiment Station at Geneva, New York, particularly Michael Fordon, were critical in the earliest stages of research. Fordon's colleagues at the Croch Library at Cornell University, particularly Evan Fay Earl, were also extremely helpful and patient. Olga Shaposhnikova, a postgraduate student working on her doctorate in viticulture from the University of Odessa and completing a year of work at the Geneva Experiment Station, was helpful in describing some of the idiosyncrasies of the Ukrainian education system, and she shared information about the physiography of the region of Ukraine where the Frank family lived.

Mr. John Babcock provided remembrances of Dr. Frank and the vigor of the man even into his eighties. John and his wife, Doris, were longtime friends of Dr. and Mrs. Frank and had important insights into their relationship and the doctor's motivation and sincerity. Robert Hutton of Alexandria, Virginia, also shared his experiences with Dr. Frank and provided translation of documents written in Russian. His knowledge of Russia and the Ukraine allowed deeper understanding of what the Frank family had endured and survived. Darmon Gleason was a neighbor and worked with Dr. Frank during the Gold Seal years, and he shared his experience and recollections of working side by side with Dr. Frank and with Eugenia Frank once Vinifera Wine Cellars was established.

Mike Elliot, Eric Frey, Peter Bell and Morton Hallgren—all winemakers under Willy Frank—were helpful in the recollections of the winery and its operations. Their thoughts and those of Mark Veraguth provided insight into the days of the fledgling and patchwork operations of Vinifera Wine Cellars. Kevin Zraly provided more firsthand accounts of Konstantin Frank and the winery operations in the early 1970s. His time was very much appreciated and helped to fill in my impression of Konstantin Frank as a man. Hudson Cattell opened his prestigious memory and allowed the use of a recorded interview with Dr. Frank, as well as provided valuable criticism along the way.

It is most important to mention up front the contribution of Fred Frank. This book is, to a large extent, a product of his enthusiasm for his family's story. Fred spent many hours answering questions, going through files, suggesting resources and people to contact. Mrs. Lena Schelling, Dr. Frank's youngest sister, was also a helpful source of information. Lena was the Frank family photographer and recorded much of their life in Ukraine and the flights to Austria and Bavaria in photos that she enthusiastically shared—each has its own story and context. She also agreed to their reproduction in this book. Appreciation must also be extended to Ms. Erin Flynn of Dr. Frank's Vinifera Wine Cellars' staff and to James Gavacs of Ettore Winter Studio for their help with the images in the book.

Given that I am not a wine expert, I relied heavily on the help and guidance of many people. Mark Veraguth, the head winemaker at Vinifera Wine Cellars, was extremely helpful in understanding the history of the winemaking operation, the unique problems facing winemakers and the ever-present management challenges of cellar operations. Eric Frey, Peter Bell, Morten Hallgren and Barbara Frank provided needed guidance and education on the technical questions about wine and winemaking. Eric Volz, vice-president of Vinifera Wine Cellars and another grandson of Dr. Frank, was very helpful in understanding the vineyard operations. Additionally, his personal recollections of the many days spent working with his father, Walter, and Dr. Frank provided a unique glimpse into not only life with Dr. Frank but also the life and work of Walter Volz.

Among the most memorable experiences were the several meetings with Margrit Frank. Her recollections of her life with Willy and her children, as well as sharing family photos and memories with me, were critical to pulling the details of the Frank family into focus. It was a privilege to be invited into the Frank family if only as an occasional observer. It is my fervent hope that this book honors their generosity and trust.

My work has benefited from the attention and efforts of Victoria Clement and Laura Dyson, who provided editorial assistance while the book was being written, and especially Andrea Ronaldi, who read and critiqued chapters in their near-final forms. Andrea's knowledge of wine and enthusiasm for the project were valuable and are much appreciated. I also want to thank Ms. Whitney Landis, Ryan Finn and the staff of The History Press for their enthusiasm and support of the project. This book is a reflection of the cooperation and help I received at every turn.

The most difficult part of the writing was deciding what to leave out. Many people came forward to offer their experience, knowledge and, frequently, anecdotes of Konstantin or Willy. There were too many for all to be included in this book. There are also numerous stories that have inevitably changed in the retelling and in the process of being passed around. Many of these have appeared in print numerous times and sometimes include claims that have been difficult to verify. Sorting these out has been a challenge. The information contained in this book represents my efforts to confirm the stories with primary sources wherever possible. In some places where this was not possible, I leave it to the reader to decide. Any errors or shortcomings in the book are entirely my own.

Part I

TO AMERICA

K onstantin Frank stepped from the Greyhound bus into the cool April night and carefully surveyed the dark city street around him; it was late, and after the eleven-hour bus ride from Manhattan, he was stiff and restless. He had come to Geneva, in central New York, on a gamble to find work at the New York State Agricultural Experiment Station. He had written to the station offering his experience and knowledge; in return, he received a discouraging letter suggesting that his skills would be better suited to California than New York and offering no hope of a job in Geneva. Frank had plenty of experience with bureaucracies living in Soviet Russia, and he knew that often one had to push against a closed door to be allowed inside. Despite the station's disappointing response, he had used some of his limited funds to purchase a bus ticket and traveled to Geneva. He was determined to find work in his field and was convinced that the experiment station would welcome him if he could get past the bureaucrats and speak directly to the scientists. He settled into a room in an inexpensive guesthouse a short walk from the Greyhound station; ate some of the food that his wife, Eugenia, had packed for his trip; and lay down to sleep. In the morning, he would walk to the Geneva station and introduce himself. Something good would come from this trip—it had to.

Frank was of average height and weight. His most remarkable features were his broad shoulders and the weathered skin that suggested a life spent working outdoors and gave little hint of his academic life. He would soon turn fifty-four years old. World War II had been over for seven years. As a newcomer to the United States, he was at some disadvantage: he spoke no English, his credentials were from another country and he had no professional contacts. But he was responsible for his family, which had recently grown from his wife and three adult children to include his wife's mother and brother, and he was ambitious and possessed a driving work ethic. He would do what it took to meet his obligations and satisfy his own professional goals.

However, work was hard to come by in 1952, when the unemployment rate in the United States hovered around 6.5 percent. The end of the war had brought home countless soldiers looking for civilian work and also displaced many of those who had worked in the wartime manufacturing effort. There were also thousands like him, displaced refugees looking to start new lives in America. He understood that there was no work for an agricultural scientist in Manhattan, but he believed that in the right place, the value of his education and experience would open doors. The trip to Geneva had used a good portion of his savings, but the experiment station offered the best hope of work in his field. He was confident that he would find men of science with similar interests and focus who shared a common interest and, at least, the language of science. If this effort were to fail, if he found no suitable employment here, he would have little choice but to return to Germany and take one of the offers of work he had turned down before leaving.

The next day was sunny but cold—a bright, crisp spring morning. He dressed in his best suit, and with his cardboard portfolio of documents in Russian and German under his arm, he walked through downtown Geneva toward the station. It had been a hard winter in central New York, but the spring had been mild and promising, as all springs tend to be. As the streets of the little downtown gradually gave way to the tree-lined residential streets of the village, yards were dotted with spring flowers and the first golden green new leaves were just noticeable overhead. Konstantin appreciated the neat, well-kept wood-frame homes as he walked to the station. Men were leaving the neighborhoods for work, and children were walking to school, while their mothers watched them go from their front porches. This place showed no sign of war or want. As Konstantin walked up Castle Street, the small city lots gave way to large treed lots with long, curving driveways leading to gracious brick homes. The farther he walked up the hill, the larger and more impressive the houses became. Every house had a car in the driveway—some even had more than one. The promise of spring seemed to unfold into something more; in America, there was so much of everything. Certainly there was a place for him and his family.

Geneva is a small city in central New York built on the site of Kanadesega, the capital of the Seneca Indian nation. The Native Americans had established sizable farms and orchards in the area long before the Europeans arrived. The earliest white settlers, noticing the quality and abundance of the Indians' crops and produce, were soon clearing land for new orchards and farms. Agriculture, especially fruit farming, soon became the most important economic activity in the region. As early as 1817, nurseries and orchards were advertising their products in local papers.[1] The area surrounding Geneva was described in one 1846 report as one continuous orchard and nursery for many miles around.[2] This rich agriculture led to a series of technical innovations and the foundation of a few notable family fortunes in the first decades of the nineteenth century. These wealthy families built some of the remarkable homes still found in Geneva today, where period architecture has been carefully preserved.

The village was first incorporated in 1806 and grew as an important economic center in the region, primarily as a market and shipping point for the agricultural produce. Seneca Lake and, later, the Erie Canal connected Geneva to both the downstate markets surrounding New York City and the western frontier markets of Buffalo and beyond. When the railroad arrived in Geneva in the 1850s, manufacturing grew in importance in part because of the transportation possibilities but also due to the nineteenth-century American entrepreneurial drive. Factories producing everything from boilers and stoves to church organs and farm equipment were established and thrived for a time. The railroad eventually replaced the canals as the mode of choice for moving goods to market given the perishable nature of agricultural products, particularly fruits and vegetables that favored the quicker means to market.

By the 1950s, much of the early manufacturing had been shut down in the face of changing demand, industry consolidation and competition, but agriculture remained as an important, even central economic activity. The early importance of farming to the region and the state was underscored by the creation of the New York State Agricultural Experiment Station at Geneva, commonly called the Geneva Experiment Station. It was originally established by the New York state legislature in 1880 "for the purpose of promoting agriculture in its various branches by scientific investigation and experiment."[3] Although established as an independent institution, it eventually was brought under the umbrella of Cornell University. By the end of the 1940s, all animal and livestock studies had been moved to Cornell University in Ithaca, New York, and the station focused its attention strictly on horticultural research. Since fruit was a major agricultural product in New York, the station had a large and active research program for fruit, berries and grapes. It was the work with grapes, or viticultural science, that drew Konstantin Frank to Geneva.

Although his prospects were uncertain, Konstantin was a motivated man. He had already lived through turbulent and dangerous times that had led his family to leave Europe to find a better life. In America, he believed, his family could live in peace, and his children would be free and able to choose their own way in life. After the years of the Russian Revolution, the repression of Stalin's Soviet government, the devastation of two world wars and the loss of family, property and freedom, peace and opportunity were the greatest hopes for his family. So far, the arc of his life had ranged from a privileged childhood in Ukraine to professional success in the Soviet Union, flight from Russia to Germany and, most recently, near destitution and refugee status in New York City. As changeable as his life had been to date, his life in the land of opportunity would prove to be equally unpredictable.

His most important and lasting work still lay before him. Over the next decade, Dr. Frank would discover the work that would define his life and legacy in America. He would demonstrate new possibilities for viticultural convention and, perhaps most importantly, challenge the status quo for that science. He would overcome significant social and technical obstacles to reveal an entirely new era of potential to the wine industry in the eastern United States and beyond. Within twenty years, he would be at the center of an entirely new trend in wine production in the country. He would become well known in the wine business, famous in some circles and somewhat infamous in others—known by his friends and detractors alike as stubborn and driven to succeed. The source of that unyielding ambition and his indomitable vision is best understood through the story of his past.

Life in Russia

Frank was one of ten children born into a wealthy ethnic German family in the Russian Ukraine.[4] Established in Russia for four generations, the ethnic Germans had maintained their language and customs after more than a century and had become a class of wealthy landowners and professionals in their adopted homeland. Like many of the Germans, the Franks owed much of their success to the czars and their policies, which had induced the first waves of German immigrants to settle the Ukraine. Among the early German immigrants was Nikolaus Frank, who came to the Ukraine in 1809 to help found the settlement of Franzfield.[5] Members of the extended Frank family were also among the founding families in the colonies of Landau, Speier, Karlsruhe and Selz. Nikolaus Frank was born in 1769 in Ottersheim/Gemersheim, Rheinpfalz, Germany. Nikolaus and his first wife, Christina, had three children: Margaretha, Joseph and Barbara. After the death of Christina, Nikolaus Frank married Elizabeth in 1811; she died shortly after the marriage. These frequent deaths suggest how difficult the early days on the steppes of the Ukraine were for the immigrants in general and women in particular. His third wife, Maria Lutz, brought three children from a previous marriage— George, Johann and Katharena—all of whom were adopted by Nikolaus, as was the custom of the times.[6] Young George Frank would grow up to marry Elizabeth Feist, and one of their children was Damian Frank.[7]

Damian eventually became a successful civil engineer and was eventually made the regional manager of the Ukrainian railroad. The Frank family had done well, acquiring large landholdings and becoming important members of the community by the end of the nineteenth century. The extent of Damian's real estate allowed him to rent some of his land to farmers in return for half of the crop, a standard practice at the time in those parts. On the remaining land, he employed help to care for his prized livestock and raise crops, including grapes for making wine. When Damian married Stanislava Petroskawa, the daughter of a wealthy merchant from Poland, their union was likely as strategic as it was romantic. Her family owned general stores that served the agricultural

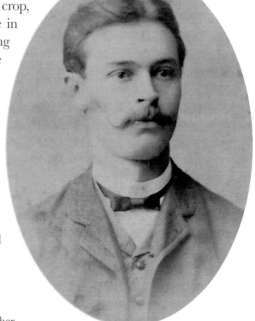

Damian Frank, Konstantin Frank's father.

communities and imported goods from abroad to stock them. Many of their stores were the only places to purchase goods for many miles. The import business was a profitable operation. The Petroskawas imported everything from food to fabric and building materials, as well as other items not found on the steppes of the Ukraine.

The joining of these two prosperous and well-connected families would have strategic business and political implications. The wealthy Frank family had connections that extended into the czar's inner circle, and they enjoyed the privileges of social rank and distinction. The Petroskawas had international connections, as well as established networks throughout Europe. The newlyweds enjoyed a privileged life, with servants and the trappings of wealth and power. Damian Frank enjoyed showing livestock at the local agricultural fairs and won competitions for the quality of his animals. It was said that he indulged his interest in livestock competitions by purchasing known winners from England and France and then showing them locally.[8]

On July 4, 1899, Stanislava gave birth to Konstantin Damian Frank. He was one of eventually ten children, only five of whom survived to adulthood.

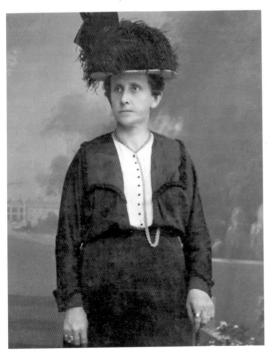

Stanislava Frank, Konstantin's mother.

The family had been in the Ukraine for four generations, but like most of their neighbors, the Franks were still "German" at heart, maintaining their language and customs in the home. The Frank children enjoyed equally privileged childhoods, with the best of comforts and education. Pictures of young Konstantin show a serious boy with a piercing, focused look in his eyes and a firmness in his jaw that suggest the character of the man he would become. By the age of twelve, he was enjoying work in the vineyards, and by fifteen, he had made his first wine.

Even as a boy, he conducted experiments with grapes and other plants and was engaged in early winemaking experiments. Konstantin would later recall being introduced to wine by an uncle: "It was 1906 in Strasbourg at a festival; my uncle gave me two glasses of wine. I became drunk and he taught me a bad Russian word. I repeated it and my mother nearly fainted from shock. Since then I have been interested in wine."[9] As a boy, he also witnessed the loss of his father's *vinifera* vines to the scourge of phylloxera as it spread across Europe. This was a formative experience. He would recall the experience and the solutions many times in later years.

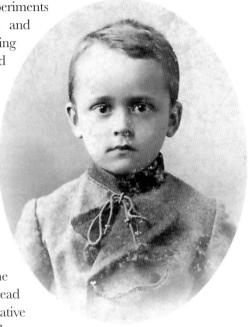

Young Konstantin Frank, date unknown.

"The Withering Disease"

Phylloxera is a pale, yellow, nearly microscopic insect that lives in soils, feeding on roots and the leaves of grapevines. It was originally found in eastern North America, where the native varieties of grapes coevolved with the pest and so are resistant to it. The *Vitis vinifera* grape varieties that grew in the Frank vineyards had no such exposure and, accordingly, no such resistance. Phylloxera attacks on the roots of grapevines cause deformations that, in turn, are subject to fungal infections. The deformations, or galls, girdle the root and cut off the flow of nutrients and water, causing the vine to wither and die. The phylloxera nymphs often survive the winter in the vineyards in the galls, within leaves or on the underside of bark on the vine roots. In the spring, the nymphs emerge and set about their work once again, making them a particularly difficult pest to eradicate. Phylloxera was introduced in France in the latter part of the nineteenth century, probably on botanical samples (not necessarily grapevines) brought in containers with soil from the United States. Once in Europe, it began to spread, wreaking havoc on vineyards across the continent.

Phylloxera was also the likely cause of failure for the various attempts to grow *vinifera* in the United States dating back to before Thomas Jefferson and Nicholas Longwood. In the eastern United States, plantings of *vinifera* would thrive for two or three years before the vines would begin to wither and then die. Since phylloxera was not discovered until late in the nineteenth century, it became accepted wisdom that European grapes, as the *Vitis vinifera* grapes came to be known, simply would not grow in eastern North America. The early and continued success of *vinifera* in California was commonly explained by the milder California climate. It was thought that the problem with *vinifera* in the East was the colder climate and nothing more.

Once the insect was introduced to the European soils, in the absence of any natural controls, it spread quickly. The first reported losses from the "blight" were in the Rhone region of France in 1863. As it spread across the continent, and as growers had no scientific solutions in hand, many attempts were made to develop some means by which to control the disease. Since the cause of the vine death was not known, many of these attempts were novel, including in one instance burying a live toad under each vine. One can only imagine the sudden market for live French toads that must have bloomed nearly overnight. None of these efforts worked, and eventually an estimated 60 to 90 percent of all European vineyards were destroyed.

The cause of the "withering disease" was not discovered until 1868 by J.E. Planchon, a French botanist at the University of Montpelier. The solution was developed by Charles Riley, an English-born entomologist working for the U.S. Department of Agriculture (USDA) along with Planchon. They determined that grafting the *vinifera* vine onto resistant native American rootstocks would allow the *vinifera* to survive the phylloxera now endemic to European soils. Their research and that of others led to the identification of rootstock scion combinations that could be tailored to different climates and soil conditions. For his work, Riley received the French Gold Medal and was made a Chevalier of the Legion of Honor in 1884. Konstantin Frank would soon be engaged in adapting these methods to solve the same problems in the Ukrainian vineyards.

REVOLUTION AND CHANGE

Damian and Stanislava Frank's five surviving children were Johann, Georges, Konstantin, Julia and Franz. They were raised in a comfortable home replete with servants and staff in an environment that placed a high value on education and learning. Johann became a civil engineer, working for the Ukrainian railroad like his father, and Georges became an electrical engineer. Franz would enter university but would eventually die in a Soviet work camp before ever graduating. Julia married and started her own family. While Konstantin was still a child in the Ukraine, feelings toward the ethnic Germans soured significantly. The Russian government banned German-language newspapers and periodicals, forbade priests to conduct Mass in German and, in some places, prohibited speaking German in public. The government declared that no teaching would be permitted in German and eventually began to remove German-speaking teachers from classrooms. Despite the fact that they had helped to settle the land, had brought new and successful techniques to agriculture and had contributed so much to the regional and national economies, the ethnic Germans were finding themselves unwelcome in what had become their home.

The Frank family had helped found and then served in leadership positions at several different settlements, including Franzfield, where Damian and Stanislava lived. After five generations, the Ukraine was the only home they knew. They had attempted to re-create their German homeland in the Ukraine, but the failure to assimilate into local culture and a history of institutionalized preferences and advantages had soured the native people against them. When problems rose between the royal families of Germany and Russia, the trend toward disaffection between the ethnic Germans and their adopted country grew worse.

When Russia entered World War I against Germany, many of the ethnic Germans were suspected of sympathizing with the kaiser and German interests and were rounded up and sent to German "colonies" in the lower Volga River.[10] Later, when Russia started losing the war, many were exiled to Siberia, where survival rates were quite low. The Franks and their children were spared from exile most likely because of Damian's position in the czar's railroad and their relationships with powerful czarist ministers and royalty. These were families and people of means with a great deal invested in the czarist government system. As the revolution played out, members of the Frank family fought for the czar and for the royalist form of government. When the Russian Revolution began in 1917, ethnic Germans came down on both sides of the revolution—the working-class Germans sympathized with the cause of the revolution, while the wealthy class, like the Franks, tended to fight for the White Army of the czar.

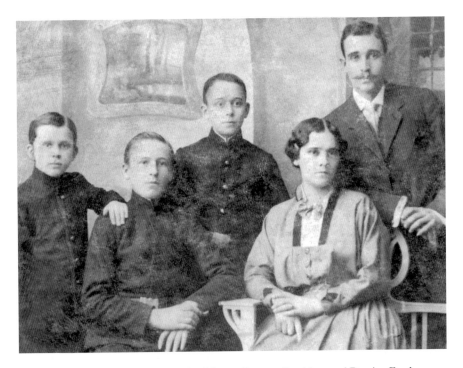

The Frank family. *Left to right*: Konstantin, Johann, Georges, Stanislava and Damian Frank.

The Franks remained loyal to the czar, and young Konstantin left school to fight in one element of the White Army, which rose in response to the Bolshevik Red Army and was composed of various factions—some were loyal to the czar, others were socialists but not communists, others fought for a democratic form of government and still others were little more than marauding criminals. As the revolution progressed, families associated with the czar were routinely arrested and sent away. During and after the revolution and civil war, still more ethnic Germans left the country; of those who stayed, many were sent into prison camps. On November 7, 1917, the communists declared landownership illegal; land was the property of the people, to be held in trust by the government. The Franks were displaced from their farms, and all of their properties were confiscated. The family moved into a large apartment in Selz.[11]

Konstantin had fought for one of the incarnations of the ill-fated White Army that was made up of those loyal to the czar, and in 1918, when the revolution was over, he was happy to leave the life of a soldier behind and return to his studies in agricultural science at Odessa Polytechnic. He quickly tried to put the war behind him, but he had not been back in his classes for long when he was expelled for being "political, not reliable."[12] The Bolsheviks did not look favorably on his service in the opposition. Konstantin returned to join the family in Selz and was fortunate to find a situation teaching in the local schools in nearby Franzfield. World War I and the revolution had depleted the number of qualified Russians for such work, and the prohibition against German teachers was, for the moment, set aside. He enjoyed teaching, but he continued to do his experiments and work with hybridizing plants. If he could not attend school, he could at least still conduct his studies. By now, Stanislava's mother and sister had come to live with the Frank family in their apartment in Selz. Like the Franks, Stanislava's family had also been dispossessed of everything and no longer had a home to call their own. Still, unlike the many other ethnic Germans who were dispossessed of land and property and forcibly relocated to other parts of the new Soviet Union, the Franks were able to avoid relocation likely due either to their family position or their desirable skills as railroad and engineering professionals.

Konstantin was still working as a schoolteacher when he married Eugenia Bartle in 1923. In light of increasing pressure from the government on

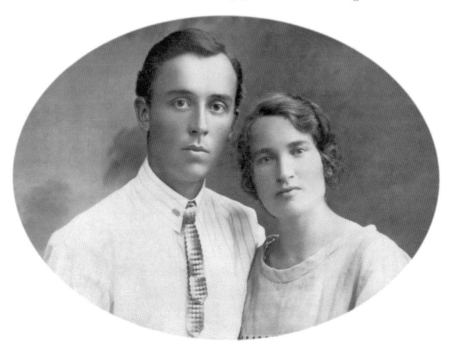

Konstantin and Eugenia, date unknown.

German-speaking Russians, and along with the ever-present risk of a renewed ban on ethnic German teachers, Konstantin and Eugenia knew that his teaching career was always going to be uncertain. He missed his formal agricultural studies, even though he had continued to conduct his own experiments and studies for years, and Eugenia encouraged him to reapply to school to complete his degree in agriculture. Perhaps the college would readmit him after so many years, and the expulsion would no longer matter. Certainly there was a critical need for agricultural expertise in the new Soviet Union. Sure enough, in 1925, the same year the couple celebrated the birth of their first child, Willibald Konstantin Frank, Konstantin reapplied to the Odessa Agricultural College and was accepted. He left teaching and went back to continue his studies.

LIFE IN THE USSR

In the decade following the Russian civil war, confiscation of land and property, the collapse of many institutions of the former government, food shortages and famine became serious problems in the Soviet Union. In part the shortages were manufactured by the policies of the new government that intentionally disrupted food distribution systems and markets largely to punish those deemed undesirable, such as the ethnic Germans, and to facilitate interests of the state. It is estimated that millions of ethnic Germans and native Ukrainian peasants were systematically starved in these early years. In 1924, the new state of the Volga German Autonomous Soviet Socialist Republic was formed. Oddly enough, this institution brought the Germans back into control and made, for a time, German the official language of the Ukraine. The food crises made those with modern agricultural expertise of particular value and increased the importance and opportunities for trained agricultural specialists like Konstantin Frank.

After earning his PhD in agricultural science in 1930, Konstantin Frank accepted a position as an instructor at the Agricultural School in Grossliebental. One year later, he was reassigned to a thirty-five-thousand-acre *kolchose*, or collective farm, called Lenina to assist in establishing some organization to the huge collective farm as an economic advisor and "master of cellars."[13] The collective was made up largely from the nationalized Troubetskoy estate and renamed the Troubetskoy Experimental Grape and Wine Station, a state agricultural experiment station that had once had more

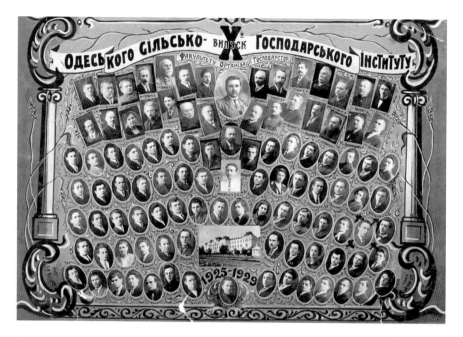

Class picture of Odessa Polytechnic, 1929. Konstantin Frank is second from the right in the third row from the bottom.

than twenty thousand acres of grapes strung along sloping land bordering the Dnieper River, where Frank was actively engaged in the restoration of the vineyards and doing viticultural research.

In 1931, Frank was reassigned once more, this time to the Russian Research Institution for Genetics and Selection in Lustdorf, where he was required by the state to conduct research on potatoes and corn (scholars' interests played no role in their assignments in the Soviet state). He enjoyed success and was publicly praised for his work by the government. While at Lenina and Lustdorf, he managed to continue his research as an assistant at the Ukrainian Agricultural Testing Station near Odessa. This work also showed promise, and in 1937, Frank was transferred back to Lenina.[14]

Shortly after his arrival at the station with his young family in tow, he was confronted once again by the effects of the phylloxera scourge—the state gave him the task of reestablishing the vineyard. Under his direction, work began to rebuild the famous Troubetskoy vineyards with grafted *vinifera* vines on phylloxera-resistant and cold-resistant rootstocks. Throughout this time, he also continued to work toward his doctorate. In the Soviet academic system, the right to the title of "doctor" is earned by completing a second research dissertation after one earns a PhD. He used the opportunity of rebuilding the Troubetskoy vineyards to conduct experiments, to test root/scion matches and to study cultivation techniques. He was able to bring students from the university to work and learn as the new vineyards were established. He and Eugenia lived in a house on the former estate with children Willibald, Brunhilde and Helene (or, as they were called, Willy, Hilda and Lena). The former duke had been allowed to remain in his castle on the grounds after the revolution and privatization of his estate, but when he died, the castle was converted to various uses, including a school that, in keeping with the new Soviet egalitarianism, was unique in that both Ukrainian and ethnic German children attended and studied side by side. The Frank children enjoyed the privileges of their father's position, living in the state-owned residence with a few servants. More practical privileges included better clothing and shoes, which they wore even in the summer, when their Ukrainian cohorts wore none.[15] As an additional privilege, Konstantin was assigned a car and a driver.

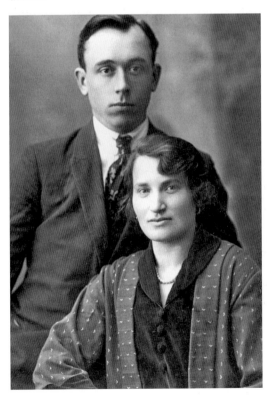

Konstantin and Eugenia, circa 1930.

Working at this huge laboratory, Konstantin enjoyed much success both in his viticulture studies and in winemaking. At the same time, his leadership, innovation and direction of the vineyards were highly praised by the Soviets, and he distinguished himself as something of an inventor. Among other things, he designed one plow to turn soil up to four feet deep and another to bury rootstocks of grapes to protect the grafts from freezing in the winter. His inventions significantly reduced the required amount of labor for these tasks and were still in wide use fifty years later. He worked for years to receive the formal recognition from the government that would have meant a substantial financial award but was never successful. His letters and the formal government responses eventually filled a thick gray cardboard portfolio that he kept for the rest of his life.[16] Several friends of Dr. Frank's who were familiar with the working of the Soviet government assumed that because he never joined the Communist Party, he was not eligible for such recognition.[17]

In the Russian famines of the late 1920s and early 1930s, many organizations and churches in the United States had made generous contributions of food and equipment to the hungry people of Ukraine and Russia. Included in the equipment gifts were several Ford tractors, which were shipped to the agricultural experiment station. Years later, Frank would recount the receipt of those tractors. To replant the vineyards, he had invented a plow to cut deep into the soil to increase root penetration of the young vines. To break the long fallow and compacted soils with gang plows, Konstantin instructed that all three tractors be connected in a direct line, one after another. When they started to pull, the last tractor to which the plows were attached bogged down, but the first tractor continued to move forward. The result was that the middle tractor was torn apart. Konstantin was charged with gross negligence and "willful destruction of state property."[18] While serious consequences were possible, he escaped with only a rebuke largely due to the intercession of

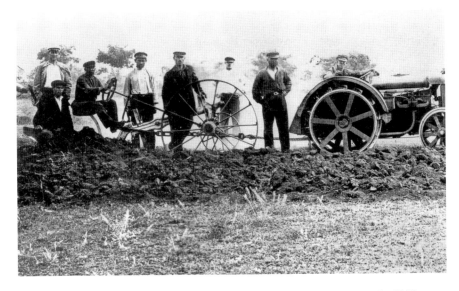

Konstantin Frank at the demonstration of his plow designed to cover rootstocks, 1928.

superiors at the institute. He would later joke that he had survived being responsible for destroying one-third of Stalin's tractors in the Ukraine.

Frank's research commanded nearly all of his attention. An apparent model of the absent-minded professor, he would frequently forget his coat or hat or completely disregard his surroundings as he pondered some question or evaluated a specimen. His youngest daughter, Lena, often accompanied her father on his rounds through the estates and on hunting and fishing trips. At the direction of her mother, she was to keep a sharp eye on her father and to collect his hat, coat, shoes or other items that he was prone to leave behind as he made his circuit. Lena diligently followed him around, offering reminders or collecting his things as he went about his day. She recalled once wading into the Dnieper River to retrieve ducks that her father had shot because he had no dog. The state provided Frank with a driver in part because of his position but also because he frequently would drive off the road if he was distracted by looking at a vineyard as he drove past or watching workers in the fields.

Over the next decade, Konstantin continued to work toward this goal through his research on the cultivation of various grape varieties, especially *Vitis vinifera* in cold climates, the foundation of his eventual legacy.[19] He had worked with French hybrids in cold climates as well, even before he was a student in the agricultural college, in his early attempts to address the phylloxera problem that had ravaged the vineyards at his family's farm. French hybrids are a cross of the *Vitis vinifera* grape with another variety, commonly a native American variety, such as *Vitis labrusca*. The cross combines the characteristics of the two through selective pollination, producing a new hybrid variety.

At the government experiment station, Frank continued to direct studies of the French hybrids until 1937, when he published a report with the World Congress for Grape Growers and Wine Makers in Tbilisi, Georgia, Caucasus. In it, he condemned French hybrids as a serious menace to the grape and wine industry, claiming that the hybrid crosses did not have the resistance to disease (most notably phylloxera) that the native varieties had and did not produce a wine that approached the quality of pure *vinifera*. He found that any rootstock with even a trace of *vinifera* was likely to have, at least, a reduced resistance to the phylloxera. His experience with the French hybrids would color his views and actions for the rest of his life. Going forward, he devoted his efforts to growing *vinifera* in the cold climate of the Ukraine. In 1939, Frank was invited to Tairov Agricultural Institute to complete work on his doctorate, which was awarded after two years of research supervised

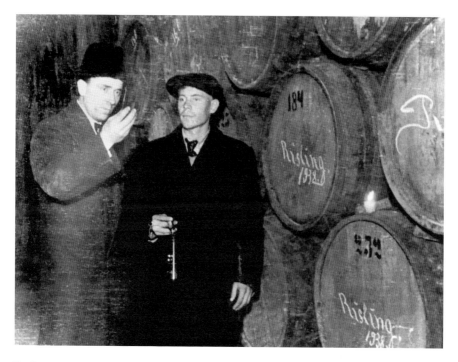

Dr. Frank in the wine cellar at the Lenina collective farm, part of the former Troubetskoy estate, 1939.

by Professor Helnik. Upon graduation, he returned to his work as technical director of the Lenina farm.[20]

Surviving World War II

In August 1939, the Soviet Union and Nazi Germany signed a non-aggression treaty. At the time, it seemed logical that both Hitler and Stalin wanted to avoid war between their respective countries. Such an agreement seemed to be in the interest of both nations. Nazi Germany would have some assurance that it would not have to contend with an eastern front (at least until it was ready), and the Soviet Union could buy some time to prepare for what it must have suspected would eventually come. Known as the Molotov-Ribbentrop Non-Aggression Pact, it included a secret agreement to return to Russia much of those portions of eastern Europe that it had given up in the treaty with Germany at the end of World War I. What Stalin could not have known was that plans for the German attack on the Soviet Union were already underway in Berlin. Throughout this time, the Soviet repression of the ethnic Germans continued. Hitler's attack on the Soviet Union in June 1941 entirely disregarded the pact, catching the Russians off guard and making the suspicion of the ethnic Germans even greater.[21]

Deportations and arrests of ethnic Germans in the Soviet Union escalated, and Frank's siblings were caught up in the new wave of repression. In 1941, Johannes Frank was arrested in Odessa and was never heard from again. Franz, the youngest of the Frank children, was arrested and deported to work camps in Siberia, where the subsistence diet and hard work eventually led to his death. Georges Frank was drafted into the Russian army in 1941; he was later captured by the Germans and allowed to join a Russian insurgent army led by disaffected Soviet general Andrey Vlasov, to whom the Germans had given the means to raise an army from captured Russians to fight against Stalin.[22] Vlasov had collaborated with Hitler to create an internal threat to Stalin's army that the insurgents fought with little success. Vlasov's liberation army was more of a propaganda ploy than an actual military force, but there was some combat in early 1945 in which some of Vlasov's commanders had a change of heart and turned their weapons on their Nazi collaborators. Vlasov eventually escaped both the Germans and the oncoming Russian Red Army and surrendered to the U.S. Army in May 1945.[23]

The Volga German Autonomous Soviet Socialist Republic remained in place until 1941, when Nazi Germany invaded the Ukraine. The ethnic Germans welcomed the invading *Wehrmacht* as a relief from the crushing oppression of the Soviets. The German army, heartened by the reception from the Ukrainian Germans, allowed for the return of private land and property. The residents who remained after the arrests and deportations of the previous decade returned to a semblance of the life they remembered from the days before the revolution. Priests were allowed back into the countryside to perform sacraments for the people, baptizing babies, blessing civil marriages and consecrating graves of those interred without the benefit of the church under the Soviets. The people repaired churches and prayed in public for the first time in more than twenty years. The ethnic Germans enjoyed their freedom from the repression of the Soviet machine, but it was not to last. In 1943, Konstantin's sister, Julia, and her eighteen-year-old daughter were shot dead by the Gestapo on a street in Odessa.

When the Russian army pushed the Germans back in 1943 and 1944, many of the ethnic Germans saw little choice but to retreat with the German army. Many who had not been conscripted into the Soviet army had sided with and sometimes fought for the Nazi army; still others had prospered once again under the brief German rule and had cooperated with the occupying forces. After the harsh years under Stalin's Soviet, little loyalty remained among the ethnic Germans, and all were fairly certain of their fate should they stay behind: more deportations, privation and repression. Most of the Ukrainian Germans who could not find another way to leave loaded their few belongings and began a long march out of Russia alongside the retreating German army. Some remained, either to wait for loved ones to return or because they were unable to survive the trip. Once the Russians reoccupied the Ukraine, nearly all of the Germans were rounded up and sent to Siberia, Kazakhstan, Altai Krai and other distant places. By the end of the 1940s, fewer than 5 percent of the ethnic Germans who once populated the region were still there. All in all, estimates of the number deported over twenty years are as high as 21 million. Almost none of them returned to their homes—indeed, most were never heard from again.

In 1941, after the German invasion of the Ukraine, Frank had been made the director of the agricultural institute by the occupying Germans.[24] The institute included the Lenina farm, the former Troubetskoy estate where he had been technical director. The war had ravaged the land and buildings, and Frank was charged yet again with rebuilding and restoring the farms to a productive condition. He worked on the project until 1944, when, with the Russian army approaching and fighting within earshot, Konstantin and Eugenia decided to take their children and leave the Ukraine.

They had become friendly with several of the German officers assigned to the administration of the area. One in particular, a man the Frank children would know only as Herr Hauptman, was a lover of wine and vineyards and was a frequent visitor to the Frank house. Hauptman had been in the wine business before the war and had known Konstantin for some time. They met in their new circumstances as old friends. Among Hauptman's duties was the management of the railroads and trains used to supply the German army along with the return of prisoners and wounded soldiers to Germany. As the Soviets advanced across the Ukraine, Konstantin knew that he would not be treated well when they arrived. He asked Hauptman if he could take his family out of the Ukraine on one of those trains. Despite regulations to the contrary, Hauptman agreed to allow the family to board a coal car attached to a train carrying wounded Germans soldiers away from the Russian front. He told them to bring only one suitcase each and enough food and water for three days. Frank covered the face of the coal pile with a carpet from their home, and he and his family huddled together under blankets and rugs,

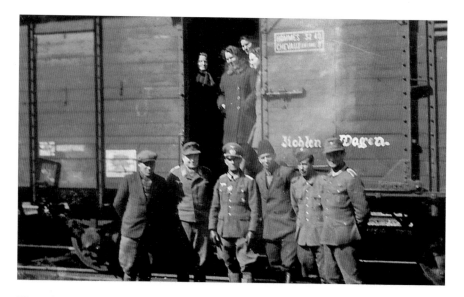

The train that bore the Frank family out of Ukraine. Eugenia, her sister, her niece and Hilda stand in the door. Captain Hauptman and Konstantin Frank are in the center in the foreground with four unknown men.

as much to protect them from the coal dust as to fend off the cold. Along the way, they were repeatedly ordered to abandon the coal car as Soviet planes approached and strafed the train. After several cold days, they arrived safely in Austria. Eventually, for escaping to the west, Konstantin and his entire family would be designated after the war as "nonpersons" by Stalin's government and their names removed from public records.[25]

Eugenia's sister, Katrina, elected to stay behind. Settling into a nice apartment that she enjoyed, she said to Eugenia, "Who is going to arrest me? I am just a woman with three children living in a small apartment."[26] Soon after the Russian army arrived, she was arrested and sent to Siberia. She lived there for more than ten years, suffering horrible deprivations and living conditions. Years later, she would write to Eugenia, who had not heard from her since the day the Franks left the Ukraine in 1944,[27] relating the harsh treatment, the poor food, the cold and the deaths of her children as a result of the unbearable conditions. The two sisters were reunited in the United States many years later.

In Austria, the Franks faced more privations at first as Russian refugees. Konstantin explained the difficulties that their nationality caused, commenting, "In Russia we were German, but in Germany we were Russian."[28] Although they stayed with family friends when they first arrived, relations soon grew strained; as soon as they were able, they moved into an apartment. Things improved for the family in Austria when Frank found work as the assistant director of state properties. His work involved managing a large farm and the restoration of another vineyard. He received a good deal of attention for implementing innovative techniques and improving equipment. His abandonment of traditional practices in favor of unfamiliar new methods drew praise from some and criticism from others. The position included a house on the farm, and the family enjoyed the new life this provided. At Christmastime in 1943, the Franks were surprised with a visit from Konstantin's brother Georges, who was enjoying a short leave from General Vlasov's nascent insurgent army. They had not heard from him since he had been drafted in 1941. Aware of the uncertainties that faced them, the family members agreed on plans for finding one another at the end of the war. At the end of Georges' short leave, the family saw him off at the train station, vowing to keep in touch. Of course, it was difficult to anticipate the events in which they would be caught up.

Shortly after moving to Austria, the Franks' son, Willy, was conscripted into the German Home Army. The Germans used members of the Romanian army to perform necessary work, and Willy was placed in charge of a unit

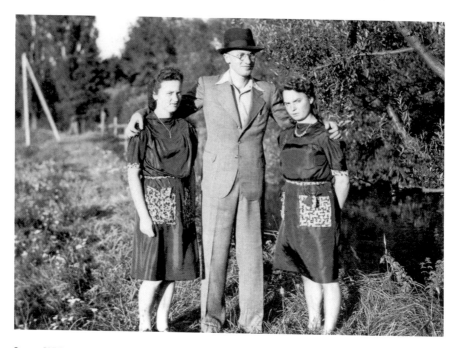

Lena, Willy and Hilda Frank, believed to be in Austria.

of Romanian sappers who were set to remove debris, restore infrastructure and eventually build defensive structures. As the Soviet army began its push into Austria, the entire unit was captured. The Romanian soldiers protected Willy by not revealing his German heritage, aware that if the Russians learned of his ethnicity, he would likely be killed. The Russians distrusted the ethnic Germans and considered them collaborators, and they treated German prisoners particularly badly. The band of Romanians was subject to fairly harsh treatment and conditions as it was. The Russians had limited supplies for themselves, so the food and blankets available to prisoners were meager at best. They were forced to march to a prison camp in Yugoslavia under the guard of Russians on horseback.

Along the way, the Romanians agreed that should the opportunity arise, they would all make a dash to escape. As they passed through a cornfield, they made their move, scattering in all directions at once. The surprised guards fired at the escaping men but were unable to see them clearly in the tall corn. Willy, remembering the tactics of escaping rabbits, zigzagged through the corn and made his way clear. He heard and saw others fall to the Russian gunfire as he ran. Shortly thereafter, he and another escapee were captured once again, this time by a band of British soldiers. He found the conditions under the British to be almost as bad as they were under the Russians. As they were marched from one camp to the next, he took the first opportunity to slip away. In short order, he was picked up once again, this time by a group of Americans. The conditions in the American prisoner of war camp were much better, and Willy Frank remained there until the war was over.[29]

Meanwhile, in Vienna, the Russians were approaching yet again. One morning, Frank heard the sound of distant cannon fire of the approaching Russian army and told the family that it was once again time to leave, this time to Bavaria, in Allied-occupied Germany. While they could expect to endure some prejudice as Russian refugees, Bavaria offered more opportunities. Frank had professional contacts there that had been established before the war. The family traveled to Bavaria, again taking only what they could carry, and Frank was able to find work again managing a farm.

When the war ended and prisoners were released, Willy started out on foot to find his family. Since food was scarce, returning soldiers and refugees like Willy had to rely on whatever people along the way could spare. In Vienna, he met a man who said that he knew the track through the mountains from Vienna to Bavaria and offered to lead the way if Willy would share his loaf of bread. Together they set off into the mountains. That night, as Willy slept, his guide slipped away with the bread; in the morning, Willy found himself alone and unsure of which way to go or when he might next eat. Eventually, with the help of farmers and others, he made his way to Bavaria and a reunion with his mother, father and sisters.

To America

Life in Bavaria after the war had some promise. Willy enrolled in the University of Nuremberg, where he would eventually earn his master's degree in business. Hilda and Helene enrolled in a business school for young women. Konstantin was hired by occupying American forces to be the superintendent of vineyards in Gradhof near Ingolsadt. This led to a series of appointments by the U.S. military government that involved the restoration of agricultural properties and facilities. With the war behind them, Konstantin and Eugenia began to look for information that might lead them to find, or at least learn the fate of, family and friends. They learned from newspaper reports that the Allies had turned General Vlasov and his soldiers over to the Russians, who reportedly hanged all of the members of the insurgent army. The Franks had no reason to believe that Georges was not among them. Red Cross records revealed no trace of Georges' wife or children. Eugenia's sister did not answer letters sent to her last known address. As far as the Franks knew, they were the only surviving members of the family; they would learn otherwise much later. Although Georges had rejoined his unit in the separatist army following his visit with Konstantin's family in Austria, he had eventually been captured by the Russians. He escaped while in transit from one prison camp to another and finally made his way to Argentina.[30] He would spend much of the next eighteen years looking for Konstantin before they made contact and were reunited once more.

The Frank family stayed in Germany for eight years, but Konstantin was not satisfied with opportunities there. Through his work with the Americans during the occupation, he had come to see the United States as the place where his family could prosper. His successes in Austria and Bavaria had brought him to the attention of authorities, and he had been offered positions in the postwar effort to rebuild the vineyards and farms of Germany. However, he envisioned life there as continuing to be difficult, with his work likely to consist only of rebuilding the property of others and with the problem of anti-Russian prejudice shadowing his efforts all the while. There was also the increasingly likely risk that talks between the Allies and Soviets would result in all former Soviet citizens being forcibly repatriated to Russia.

Possibilities for life in Canada or the United States were much more appealing. He recalled the powerful influence of the generous gifts of food and equipment that had come from America to the starving people in Russia years before. Treatment from U.S. personnel in the postwar construction period had left a positive impression, as they seemed to have nearly limitless resources at their disposal. He also had contacts in Canada and initially thought that it might be easier to immigrate there. He wanted to live in peace, pursue his experiments and teach. Under no circumstances did he want to return to the Soviet Union. Freedom for such pursuits was the foundation of American life, as Frank saw it, and he began to look for the means by which to bring his family to the United States.

With as many as 10 million refugees and displaced people in camps at the end of the Second World War, it was clear that the Allies were going to have to do something to accommodate them and manage the dissolution of internment and refugee camps scattered around Europe. At the Yalta Conference in 1945, Churchill, Roosevelt and Stalin agreed that displaced persons should be able to return to their countries of origin if they so desired. Stalin insisted that persons who at one time held citizenship in the Soviet Union would be returned whether they wanted to do so or not. Of course, the Soviet Union now occupied Poland and many eastern European countries that it did not control at the start of the war. Stalin wanted all of these people repatriated, and Churchill and Roosevelt agreed in principle.[31] Many of the people returned to the Soviet Union and the occupied countries of eastern Europe were subsequently sent to concentration camps or executed. The Franks clearly had no interest in returning to the Soviet Union and probably represented themselves as Germans to the American authorities to avoid forced repatriation.

In the United States, the Displaced Person Act of 1948 was passed and reauthorized in 1950.[32] These laws did not necessarily increase immigration to the United States but rather gave preference to persons displaced by the war and provided for an enhanced preference if they had family in the United States or had a sponsor. A sponsor had to demonstrate that the immigrant had a place to live and that there was work available for the sponsored person. The 1950 law included an allowance for up to fifty-five thousand Volksdeutschen (ethnic Germans) to immigrate to the United States provided that they were sponsored by American citizens.

In Germany, the Franks met many displaced people like themselves. Some of these people were able to find sponsors in the United States and immigrate. Once the immigrant was settled in the United States, he or she sought sponsors for the friends left behind. Many religious organizations established resources to identify sponsors and connect them with eligible immigrants. Valentin Zahorsky, a pianist and a friend of the Franks from Vienna and Bavaria, had already immigrated to the United States.[33] Working with a group of sympathetic Americans in New York City, he helped the Franks and others find sponsors who would enable them to immigrate to the United States. To immigrate, they had to show that they had a place to live, and someone had to assure the authorities that they would not be an economic burden to the government of the United States. With the help of the Zahorskys and others, the Frank family immigrated to the United States in 1951.[34] After experiencing two wars, the Bolshevik Revolution, loss of property and wealth, political repression and the deaths of so many loved ones, friends, students and neighbors, the Franks saw the United States as the embodiment of hope and promise.

A New Life

On December 15, 1951, the USNS *General R.M. Blatchford* sailed into a blustery New York Harbor.[35] On board were more than 1,200 refugees and displaced persons from fourteen eastern European countries.[36] The *Blatchford* was engaged in troop transfers in the Pacific Theater throughout World War II, but after the war, it was put to use transporting refugees from Europe to new homes in Australia and the United States. Its last trip in that capacity was to sail from Bremerhaven, Germany, to New York City. The passengers were interviewed and processed on board, but it was two days before they were finally cleared by customs officials to enter the United States. They collected their few belongings and disembarked in small groups, setting foot in their adopted country for the first time. Among the refugees were Dr. Konstantin Frank, his wife and their three grown children.

The Zahorskys had arranged a small apartment for the Franks and a job for Konstantin as a dishwasher at the Horn and Hartart Automat. Upon release from Ellis Island's immigration center, the Franks moved into the dingy apartment in Lower Manhattan.[37] The apartment was small for the five adults, infested with cockroaches and, in the midst of the New York

City winter, quite cold. Frank's job as a dishwasher on the night shift at a Horn and Hartart Automat brought in some much-needed cash and allowed him time to look for a better situation during the day. The family conserved their small savings and struggled to get along on the little money Frank was earning as a dishwasher. Eugenia had sewed much of the family's savings into the linings of Hilda's and Lena's winter coats before they left Germany. When they needed to dip into the savings, one of the girls would produce her coat, and Eugenia would rip out enough of the lining to remove the needed amount and sew the coat back up. To keep expenses low, they bought day-old bread and dried it so that it would keep longer. They would hang the bread from a clothesline in the apartment to keep the roaches away, but it had to be watched constantly to prevent the resident mice from crawling along the clothesline and eating it.[38]

The fact that none of the Franks spoke fluent English was a problem. Work was a challenge for anyone to find, but for non-English-speaking displaced persons (or "DPs," as they were increasingly and derisively called), it was especially slow in coming. Willy spoke some English that he had learned in the American prison camp and from students at the University in Nuremberg. A quick study, he was able to pick up more in relatively short order. He would take his sisters to local movies, where, for a nickel, they could sit all day, reel after reel, learning the language from the movie stars and the newsreels of the day. Konstantin and Eugenia, however, did not go to the movies, and for them the new language was a trial. Hilda and Lena eventually began to take classes to improve their English. Everyone in the family spoke at least three languages—German, Ukrainian and Russian. Konstantin spoke at least five languages—including German, Russian, Polish and French—but English was the language he needed, and he struggled to learn it.

Soon after arriving in New York, Konstantin began to look for work in agriculture, ideally conducting research, as he had in the Ukraine, but with limited financial resources and no contacts, progress was slow. He wrote letters to government agencies and universities, but after several months of effort yielded no indication that he would be able to find suitable work in the United States, he began to lose heart. Frank wrote in his letters to friends, "I left Germany in November of 1951 with my family and hope to find suitable employment in the U.S.A., if possible in an agricultural or Testing Station or on a large farm on the basis of my thirty years of practical and scientific activities in Germany and Russia. I hope to be able to be helpful to my new country."[39]

Dismayed by the lack of work and the family's dismal living conditions, he began to think about returning to Germany. He was well known in his profession there and had many longtime professional contacts and friends. Before he had left for the States, he had received several generous offers for work in prestigious positions in Germany. Perhaps one of them might still be available. Returning to Europe would be admitting defeat, though, and he had no stomach for that. Nevertheless, having found no opportunities in the land of opportunity, Frank wrote to his contacts in Germany to inquire about work.

Colleagues in Germany wrote that indeed there was work for him there but suggested that before he gave up, he should look into the New York State Agricultural Experiment Station at Geneva—noting its fine reputation and the prominence of Cornell University as an agricultural school. They pointed out that the climate and conditions of the Finger Lakes resembled those of the agricultural experiment station he had managed on the former Troubetskoy estate and that his experience and knowledge would therefore be of particular value. The Finger Lakes region in central New York was climatically comparable to the lands along the Ukraine's Dnieper River, with similar geography of sloping lands and adjacent deep water. Konstantin agreed that his academic and professional work growing *vinifera* grapes in cold climates was especially applicable. With renewed hope, he wrote to the Geneva Experiment Station seeking employment. Such was his confidence that the institution would welcome his experience and skills that the refusal letter was no deterrent. He simply got on the bus.

At home in the Ukraine, Frank had been the technical director of a large agricultural experiment station, had received honors for his work restoring and managing large collective farms, was a noted inventor of farm implements and was a leading researcher in the field of viticulture, specializing in growing wine grapes in cold climates. He arrived in the United States with no professional contacts, very little money, no English and no prospects, but he brought with him thirty years of experience, a passion for science, an indomitable confidence and a driving ambition to distinguish himself in his new homeland just as he had in the old country. Like so many of their fellow refugees, the middle-aged agricultural scientist and his wife of nearly thirty years were starting over, beginning a new life together. Sustained by the pioneer spirit of their ancestors, they intended to fully embrace the promise of America.

When Frank arrived in Geneva in early April 1952, that promise lay before him, the future shimmering with hope and possibility. At the experiment station, he was at first welcomed as a colleague who had dropped by for an expected visit. He was given a tour and introduced to some staff and researchers, relying on several German-speaking staff members to interpret for him.[40] He pressed his hosts for an employment opportunity, but they were fully staffed, and there was no position for a senior scientist with his qualifications at that time. The only work available for him was a grant-funded position studying field nursery methods, but it was, in a sense, work in his field. Frank accepted the position, anticipating that if he were present and working, better opportunities were more likely to come his way. Besides, it would allow him to get his family away from the squalid circumstances in Manhattan. It was a start.

Part II

THE FINGER LAKES

Despite the discouraging letter he had received from Cornell, Konstantin arrived unannounced at the New York State Agricultural Experiment Station in Geneva to ask for a job. No suitable professional positions were available, but presumably as a result of his willingness, his résumé and the force of his personality, a temporary position was found for him working on a grant exploring field nursery practices. Konstantin rented a room that was within walking distance of the station and began work. Whether the staff initially recognized his experience in the Ukraine with cold-weather grape production as immediately relevant to their work is arguable. He was assigned to work with Karl Dietrich Brase, a researcher interested in grafting fruit trees, under the supervision of Dr. Nelson Shaulis. The station newsletter of April 16, 1952, welcomed the new employee as a qualified scientist, announcing, "Dr. Konstantin Frank, newly-arrived from Germany, has joined the Station's Pomology Division on a temporary appointment in connection with the Stuart grant for nursery investigations. Dr. Frank had twenty years of nursery experience in Russia."[41] No mention was made of the fact that he had been the technical director of an agricultural experiment station similar to, but much larger than, the Geneva station.

Karl Brase, the man with whom Konstantin was assigned to work, was born and received his early horticultural training in Germany, eventually immigrating to the United States to work as a plant propagator at the Geneva Experiment Station and to study at Cornell University, where he received his BS (1935) and MS (1937).[42] His professional focus was on scion-rootstock relationships in fruit trees, and he eventually became recognized as an expert in this area. This common interest and shared language could have been the basis for a close working relationship, but this was not to be. Although Konstantin was grateful to be working in agricultural research, he considered his role menial, little more than that of a field laborer. In Ukraine and in Germany, he had been a respected professor and leader. He had enjoyed the benefits of his family's wealth and, later, those of an important director of the leading agricultural research institute in the Soviet Union. He had enjoyed the service of chauffeurs, household staff and an intellectually stimulating and satisfying life.

In Geneva, he found that his ideas were at best politely discounted and at worst outright ridiculed. Regardless of his credentials and professional experience, as a field assistant his work consisted of conducting and recording the research work of others, never his own. Nevertheless, he believed that any work associated with agriculture was better than washing dishes and more likely to provide other chances in his field. He remained in Geneva, working on the grant, investigating nursery methods and waiting for the next opportunity.

After a short time in his rented room, he was invited to live in the home of another Russian emigrant, Alexander Brailow, then a winemaker working for Gold Seal winery, located on Keuka Lake. Brailow had heard of the Russian who had appeared at the experiment station looking for work and sought Konstantin out to share his home. Each weekend, Konstantin would ride the bus from Geneva to New York City, sleeping much of the eleven hours each way to enjoy a few home-cooked meals and to collect the food Eugenia prepared for him to take back. He eschewed restaurants not only because they were too expensive but also because he took little pleasure in the food. Instead, he lived each week on Eugenia's sandwiches until they were gone, and then he would eat cereal and milk until it was time to go back to New York and stock up again.

By June 1952, Konstantin had found suitable living arrangements and was able to bring Eugenia to Geneva. Their children—Willy, Hilda and Lena—all elected to remain in New York. Willy had found work selling photographic equipment and was doing well. He was introduced by mutual friends to Margrit Totzke, and they were soon engaged. In a matter of months, Hilda and Lena had met Walter Volz and Edwin Schelling, their respective future husbands. Walter Volz was a machinist in New Jersey with steady work. Edwin Schelling was building a successful insurance business in the Catskills of New York. The Frank children were going about their lives.

Despite its frustrations, working at the experiment station kept Konstantin engaged in the field and provided opportunities to meet and talk with people, including fellow scientists and vineyard owners. He took every opportunity to meet and talk with fellow scientists and to look for more appropriate work. His work at the station allowed for him to attend conferences and meetings held in the region. In 1952, he had an article published in the *American Fruit Grower*, "The Phylloxera Menace in the Vineyard." Dr. Frank recalled some years later that Fred Taylor of Taylor Wine Company, Mr. Howell of Pleasant Valley Wine Company and Charles Fournier of Gold Seal all had expressed some interest in his ideas and had initially had some interest in having him work as a consultant to their companies. However, the offers never materialized, and Frank later wrote in a letter to colleagues at the United States Department of Agriculture that "the scientists at Geneva discouraged them saying it could not be done at all."[43] The bitterness of that turn of events could still be read between the lines of his letter written more than twenty years later. His disappointment in that lost opportunity and the role of the senior staff at the station, whether real or perceived, may have planted the seeds that would grow into the resentment and pugnacity that would mark Frank's relationship with many of the "Genevans," as he would later refer to them.

The Franks set up housekeeping in Geneva not far from the grounds of the experiment station. Although the salary was small, the Franks were frugal by nature and experience. They took pleasure in the social life of the local church and in the natural beauty of the Finger Lakes. The Franks were devout Catholics. In the Soviet Union, religion was banned, and observance, if any, was secret. In Geneva, they were able to join a local parish and worship freely. Eugenia was able to enjoy singing in the choir again. They both enjoyed attending Mass and participating in the sacraments. These were not small freedoms to people who had experienced the repression of Stalin's Soviet Union. Konstantin had always enjoyed hunting and fishing, and the region provided many opportunities to pursue both for leisure and the occasional meal. The beauty and abundance of the land around Geneva was a fitting backdrop to their new experience of American liberty, but it also was a land rich with opportunity for the ambitious immigrant. Konstantin quickly grew to love his adopted country and, in time, would become a citizen and fervent patriot.

Geneva is located in that region of central New York known as the Finger Lakes, which acquired the name because early mapmakers saw some similarity between the five largest lakes and the splayed fingers of a hand.

They are the result of the last two glacial periods of Earth's history, one about 2 million and the other about 13,000 years ago. The surrounding area is composed of physical features formed by those periods—the telltale land forms composed of the sediments deposited as the glaciers retreated northward. The great weight of continental glaciers (up to thousands of feet thick) gouged wide and deep valleys marking the direction of the glacial movement. Eventually, the glaciers receded, leaving behind large deposits of glacial till that effectively cut off the original drainage to the south and caused the valleys cut by the glaciers to fill up with water until they overflowed and new drainage patterns were established. These flooded valleys are the modern Finger Lakes. The resulting landscape was ideal for agriculture: fertile soils, good water and a generally conducive climate.

The Finger Lakes region has supported fairly diversified agriculture for a long time. A number of large Native American towns and many villages were established and flourished in the area under the auspices of the Iroquois nation. The powerful Iroquois were able to keep western European expansion largely in check until well into the eighteenth century in part because of their military capability but also, to some extent, because of their strategic choices in allowing some controlled and limited European settlement. The Europeans who first inhabited the region soon realized and made the most of its rich agricultural potential. While grains, fruit, dairy and livestock did well throughout the area, the problem facing these early farmers was how to move their produce to distant markets in Buffalo and New York City over the hilly and heavily forested country. The presence of lakes and rivers allowed for inexpensive transportation, but it was slow and required frequent loading and unloading. Also, the orientation of most navigable waterways was north–south, and the markets were largely to the west and east. The era of canal construction eventually boomed, as entrepreneurs and governments sought to increase the flow of goods between growing cities like Buffalo and New York City and the ports that lay beyond them. The Erie Canal began operations in 1825 and opened major markets for the farmers of the Finger Lakes.

Then, as now, shipping bulky, raw agricultural products to distant markets was not particularly economical. Shipping unprocessed, bulky farm produce is expensive, and the low market value of commodity crops does not allow for much profit. Shipping perishable goods such as fruit and raw dairy products risks heavy losses from spoiling and damage during shipping. The best margins for farmers are provided through products of less bulk, ones that can travel well and have higher values at the market. These economics led to the development of local milling industries, cheese factories, the canning of vegetables and preserves and, eventually, wine and spirits. Such processing of raw agricultural products to forms that would travel better and bring higher market returns justified investment in growing industries and improvements in transportation.

Native varieties of grapes, like many other fruits, did well in the glacial till of the region, but shipping fragile grapes was usually accompanied by significant losses caused by damage and spoiling. In 1869, two unconnected but important events occurred that were to have significant impacts on the grape growing business. First, H.L. Blowers devised a method to ship fresh grapes in specially made boxes without significant losses. Perhaps more importantly for the Finger Lakes, Thomas Bramwell Welch, a Methodist minister and dentist, invented a method of making and preserving grape juice so that no fermentation would occur. Shipping grapes as juice was an even more cost-effective way to transport grapes. A lifelong teetotaler, Welch promoted his grape juice product as a healthy, nonalcoholic alternative to wine, and it was his hope that consumers would give up wine and substitute grape juice. The grape juice business was successful but remained largely a sideline for Welch and his family until 1893, when sales reached a point that allowed him to devote his energy to the business full time. In 1896, the Welch's Grape Juice Company moved its operations from New Jersey to the Finger Lakes of New York. Welch's grape juices were made from native Concord grapes, and the success and growth of the company drove the planting of more and more acres of grapes. Even today, more than two-thirds of the grapes grown in New York State, an estimated 100,000 tons each year from more than twenty thousand acres of vines,[44] are Concord grapes grown primarily for juice and jelly.

THE WINE GRAPES

Interest in growing grapes and producing fine wine in America is at least as old as the presence of Europeans in the New World, but the only extended successes of any note had been limited to the West Coast, primarily California. Early wines from the many native grape varieties were generally not appreciated by knowledgeable wine drinkers. Efforts to produce table wines similar to those produced in Europe using native varieties were disappointing and enjoyed only limited success at best. The native *labrusca* varieties, like Concord, developed relatively low sugar content and therefore produced little alcohol in fermentation. To overcome this, alcohol was added directly or sugar was added to foster fermentation and the production of alcohol, but the native grapes also lacked the necessary acid to balance the unfermented or residual sugar, resulting in particularly sweet wines.

Near the turn of the twentieth century, as grape production grew, winemakers solved this problem by importing California wine in bulk rail cars to blend with the juice from the *labrusca* grapes, adding acid to the mix, balancing the residual sugar and hiding the undesirable "foxy" tastes. The term "foxy" refers to the grapey flavor of wine considered undesirable by most wine enthusiasts but favored by children. Think of the grape juice you probably enjoyed as a child, and you will have a sense of the flavor. The term itself is probably derived from the early English settlers, who called the native grapes "fox grapes," referring to the larger size of the native berries compared to familiar European grapes. These additives were necessary, along with the addition of California bulk wine shipped in railroad cars to New York, to produce a consistent inexpensive, sweet and more alcoholic wine.

Prior to the Volstead Act being signed into law by President Wilson in 1919, table wines accounted for three out of every four gallons of wine made and sold in the United States. There were more than 2,500 wineries of various sizes throughout the country.[45] Many of these were producing wines for local communities of mostly European immigrants who had grown up with wine as a staple of life in their native countries. The Eighteenth Amendment and the Volstead Act effectively shut the industry down; fewer than 100 wineries survived the thirteen years of Prohibition. By the time the "Noble Experiment" was ended by the passage of the Twenty-first Amendment in 1933, the wine industry had been decimated. The market for table wines was largely reduced to those who could afford the relatively high prices of imported wine. The Volstead Act allowed individuals to make wine for their own consumption, and home winemakers were frequently immigrants who brought the culture of wine and winemaking with them from their native countries.

After Prohibition, the wine industry was dominated by large companies that produced primarily cheap, sweet wine from *labrusca* and hybrids that required added sugar and alcohol. The market for these wines was essentially the same market targeted by the makers of liquor, with whom some of the larger wine companies were in direct competition. As long as they could produce these sweet, highly alcoholic beverages and sell them for less than spirits, the business was profitable. Frequently, the wine production was owned by the same companies producing the distilled spirits whose focus was on marketing cheap alcoholic beverages, not on producing quality table wines.

The United States had no "wine culture" such as that enjoyed by Europeans, and as a result, after Prohibition, drinking wine was often seen as synonymous with skid row bums or "winos," who preferred the wine over liquor because it was sweet and cheap. This segment of the market had little concern with body and nose, mouth "feel," food pairings and whether or not to decant. In this post-Prohibition environment, there was little commercial interest in growing varieties that would produce quality table wine.

Although numerous attempts had been made to grow European varieties, all *Vitis vinifera*, beyond the West Coast, ended in failure. Even the most successful generally enjoyed only a few seasons of production before the "withering disease," phylloxera, found them and wiped them out. The *vinifera* had no ability to resist the phylloxera like the native varieties had. Before the cause of the withering disease was known, which was not until the latter half of the nineteenth century, it was the commonly accepted knowledge that you could not grow European grapes in America, except in California. Of course, *vinifera* were being grown successfully in California because there was no phylloxera present in the native soils, but that would not be known for decades to come; eventually, the withering disease would spread to the West Coast.

There are many different varieties of grapes, including *Vitis vinifera*, *Vitis labrusca*, *Vitis riparia*, *Vitis rotundifolia* and so on. Of all grape varieties, particular members of the family of *Vitis vinifera* produce grapes that are said to make the best wine. The name *vinifera* means "wine bearing grape." In the past, a few of these were commonly called the "noble grapes": Cabernet Sauvignon, Pinot Noir, Merlot, Chardonnay, Riesling, Sauvignon Blanc and Pinot Gris. The term has fallen out of use for several reasons, primarily because it is simply too exclusive. Still, while there are many thousands of varieties of *vinifera* grapes, it is still only a relative handful that produce excellent wines that reflect the soils and climate of a particular region. The so-called noble varieties might be more of a function of having been grown in France, where winemaking developed into a product of tradition and commerce, unlike most other places. In the United States, *vinifera* varieties are often referred to as "European grapes" or even "California grapes" to distinguish them from the more common and locally more hardy native varieties such as *Vitis labrusca*, *Vitis riparia* and *Vitis rotundifolia*.

The modern wine industry in New York enjoys several key centers of production. The Long Island Sound provides the tempering effect that makes Long Island a key winemaking area in the state. The regions along Lake Erie are clustered in the narrow band of land that enjoys some moderation in climate from the lake. In the Finger Lakes region, the wine industry is centered largely on the largest lakes—Cayuga, Seneca, Keuka and Canandaigua—and, to some extent, Honeyoe and Conesus Lakes. These deep natural lakes provide what is called the "lake effect," which tempers the extremes of weather and makes for a more conducive grape climate, coupled with good soil and sufficient sun and rain, which are characteristics that contribute to the essential character of a Finger Lakes vineyard.[46]

The French refer to the characteristics that enable a place to impart its unique character to a wine as its "terroir," a literal reference to the land on which particular grapes are grown. The definition of these special places can reach a fairly high degree of refinement. As a result, these distinctive areas can be quite small in area—indeed, some are so small that they include only a portion of a field that has unique characteristics of soil, slope and an aspect that might be found to be unique and worthy of its own designation. For example, there are more than 340 distinct, named vineyards with legal descriptions and restrictions that make up the appellation d'Origine Controlee, known worldwide as the Champagne region of France. Such designations are definitive and difficult to come by but can be an important factor in distinguishing wine quality, character and price—and some are only a few acres in size. To further define the terroir, the designation may be limited to a particular type of grape. Such a designation notes that, in principle, the unique character of this wine from this place cannot be duplicated anywhere else because of the specific terroir.

It could thus be argued that any wine growing region is a unique combination of soils, slope and climate where one or several varieties of grapes would enjoy cultural advantages over some other variety. Certainly New York State, due to its size and physical variability, has regions of wine production that differ quite a bit from one another. Perhaps one area might enjoy fewer climatic extremes or predictably milder winters, whereas another might have soils of particular drainage and depth. Since 1987, the Finger Lakes area has enjoyed the distinction of its own appellation or American Viticultural Area (AVA). In the 1950s, of course, little thought had been given to such matters.

PHILIP WAGNER AND HYBRIDS

In 1945, Philip Wagner, owner of Boordy Wines in Maryland, visited the Geneva Experiment Station and met with Dr. Nelson Shaulis, along with a number of prominent winemakers from the region. The purpose of his visit was to continue the practice of sharing information on hybrid grape varieties that could be grown in the East and produce good wine. Wagner was an editor for the *Baltimore Sun* and a wine enthusiast. On trips to Europe, he and his wife, Jocelyn, became enamored of wine and eventually decided to try making their own, even going so far as to smuggle grape cuttings home in their luggage. With the diligence one would expect of a former newspaper reporter, Wagner researched the subject and was disappointed to learn of the history of failure associated with the *vinifera* varieties. Not to be deterred, he planted *vinifera* but eventually shifted his focus to French hybrids as a workable alternative. He began his own nursery in Riderwood, Maryland, for French hybrids and became a source of vines and, eventually, advice to home winemakers. Wagner and Jocelyn started making wine in the early 1930s, even as Prohibition was being repealed. The Volstead Act and laws stemming from the Eighteenth Amendment, which created national Prohibition, allowed individuals to make up to two hundred gallons of wine each year for personal use.

When the *vinifera* varieties failed, he started working with French hybrids. French-American hybrids were plant varieties developed by cross-pollinating the native varieties and a *vinifera* variety in an attempt to coax the most desirable characteristics of each into a new plant. The hybrid was then grafted onto a native American grape rootstock. The crosses were more cold-hardy and disease-resistant than the *vinifera* and produced better-quality wine than the native American varieties alone. A successful cross might have the cold and disease resistance of the native and the fruit characteristics of the *vinifera*, although this precise outcome is unlikely. It is more likely that some of the desired as well as some of the undesired characteristics would be expressed in the new plant. Since each attempt at hybridization can result in different combinations of the genetic material of each parent plant, thousands of hybrids needed to be made and grown to production age to assess the relative success of each combination. From these thousands of attempts, some successes occurred, but would these always represent some degree of compromise between the wanted and unwanted characteristics of the parent plants.

In 1933, Wagner authored a book entitled *American Wines and How to Make Them.* Wagner saw a market for information on home winemaking, and his book is generally credited with prompting a new post-Prohibition enthusiasm for wine and winemaking in the United States. Eventually, he was selling cuttings and information across the United States on how to make table wines in the styles of the old European wines but with using French hybrids instead of *vinifera*. During his visits to Geneva throughout the 1930s and 1940s, he brought with him documentation of the hardiness and vigor of his grapes and wine made from his French hybrid varieties to taste. Wagner had been driving north to these meetings for years to discuss the potential of French hybrids and to exchange ideas for producing good table wine. Those who would attend these meetings included, among others, Charles Fournier from Gold Seal Wines and Adhemar de Chaunac, winemaker from T.G. Bright and Company, a large winemaking operation located on the Niagara Peninsula in Ontario, as well as staff from the New York State Agricultural Experiment Station. Both Fournier and De Chaunac had long been searching for the varieties and methods to produce good table wines in the cold northern climates. Both men remembered the wines from their native France, where they received their training, and sought a cold-hardy variety that would produce wine of equal quality.

By 1945, Wagner had convinced them of the hardiness and quality of the various French hybrids that he was promoting. He brought bottles of wines to share and demonstrate that the French hybrids could produce good table wine. When World War II ended and importing cuttings and grafts from France was allowed to continue, both Fournier and De Chaunac placed orders from French nurseries. De Chaunac ordered thirty-five French hybrid varieties and four *vinifera* varieties for use in the Ontario vineyards. When these were planted in 1946 in Bright's research vineyards, George Hostetter was put in charge of the new research. The French hybrids were successful in trials, and in 1948, Bright and Company planted forty thousand vines for production.[47] Fournier and other New York wineries also began making serious commitments to the French hybrids.

At Bright in Ontario, George Hostetter continued the research into the *vinifera* vines, and by prophylactic spraying rather than waiting for signs of an outbreak, he was able to overcome the *vinifera* losses to powdery mildew encountered in the first years. This innovation led to the first successful commercial production of *vinifera* in the East. Bright released a Pinot Champagne in 1955 and a Chardonnay in 1956. The combined lake effects of Lake Erie and Lake Ontario protected the Bright's *vinifera* from the cold of the winter, and Hostetter's spraying innovations protected the grapes from the fungi of the humid summer typical in the East.

Dr. Shaulis and the scientists at the Geneva station noted the successes of Bright and Gold Seal and in 1947 began research into their own program hybridizing of grapes for wine production.[48] The wine industry and growers took note, and an enthusiastic shift toward French hybrid grapes began and was well underway by 1952, when Konstantin Frank arrived in Geneva. When Frank questioned the scientists at the station about why *vinifera* was not being grown and promoted to farmers, he was informed of the well-established belief that they could not be grown because of the cold climate. When he insisted that they could be grown, his view was discounted as uninformed. Not easily discouraged, he took his thoughts to others, including Dr. Shaulis himself. His immediate colleagues suggested that he refrain from pursuing this risky proposition, which ran counter to the views of the authorities at the station.

THE NYS AGRICULTURAL EXPERIMENT STATION AND *VINIFERA*

However, for Konstantin, the *vinifera* proposal was not at all risky or uncertain. He had been successful in growing thousands of acres of *vinifera* in a very cold, nearly subarctic climate on a commercial scale in Russia. He had studied the problem as a student and had successfully put his ideas and methods into practice as the technical director of an agricultural experiment station much larger than the one in Geneva. To Konstantin, the quality of the wine produced from *vinifera* was far superior to anything that could be made from French hybrids, and the quality alone made the effort worthwhile. To be discounted and ignored was more than he was willing to bear in silence, and so he continued to make his arguments. Dr. Shaulis disagreed with Konstantin on the question of growing *vinifera* commercially in New York. Both men were very knowledgeable and well educated in their field but had very different experiences and visions. In the end, this was not a disagreement between equals—Dr. Shaulis was the director of the viticulture program at the experiment station, while Frank was essentially little more than a field hand in a temporary grant-funded position. To complicate matters, although he was fluent in at least four languages, Dr. Frank was only just learning to speak English, though his skills were steadily improving. When making his case for *vinifera*, his passion would rise, and he would often slip into German or Russian not understood by most of the senior staff of the station.

Dr. Nelson Shaulis is widely remembered as a pioneer in viticulture and one of the developers of what is known internationally as the Geneva Double Curtain trellis system, among other innovations. Shaulis had observed that on grapevines with vigorous growth habits, shade caused by the upper growth reduced ripening in fruit set lower on the vine. The Geneva Double Curtain system involves training the grapevine branches at a ninety-degree angle from the rootstock and then training the canes downward and on wires set on either side of the row. It is widely used throughout the world for particularly vigorous varieties of grapes. Shaulis was also instrumental in developing the machinery and the vineyard systems that facilitated mechanical picking of grapes, and he even contributed to early work on climatic change in the Finger Lakes.

Although his expertise was viticulture, Shaulis probably saw grape production as just another agricultural crop—no different, really, than apples or beans. He was not known to drink or appreciate wine, and at the time of his work, the market for grapes grown in New York State was primarily for the grape juice industry and secondarily for the wine industry—therefore, that is roughly how the work of the viticulture program was apportioned. The wine business was an aftermarket concern for grape farmers in New York; grapes were grown, harvested and then sold. What happened to the grapes after they were sold was not the business of the station, at least not directly. New York grape growers were producing grapes for juice and jelly, for the market created primarily by the Welch's Corporation, and secondarily for the wine market. In any case, they were the same grapes, with no distinction being made between the different characteristics that might best suit the end product of jelly or wine. From this perspective, the station focused on where the market was and not where the market might eventually be. As a publicly funded institution, the station was charged first with serving existing agricultural activities and interests, not in pursuing new crops for which there was no market, no interest and no money to fund research. While "experiment" might have been in the station's name, there were practical limits as to how far reaching the experiments would be.

Konstantin spent a considerable amount of his spare time in the experiment station library reading the old bulletins and reports. Reading these technical bulletins helped him learn the language, particularly the technical language. He eventually found that in the past, more than 150 varieties of *vinifera* had actually been grown at the station and that one was considered to have a "high winter hardiness," the Pinot Gris; this stood in stark contrast to the principle that *vinifera* could not be grown in New York. Upon some inspection, he found that some of the original experimental vines were still growing on the grounds of the station more than forty years after they were planted.

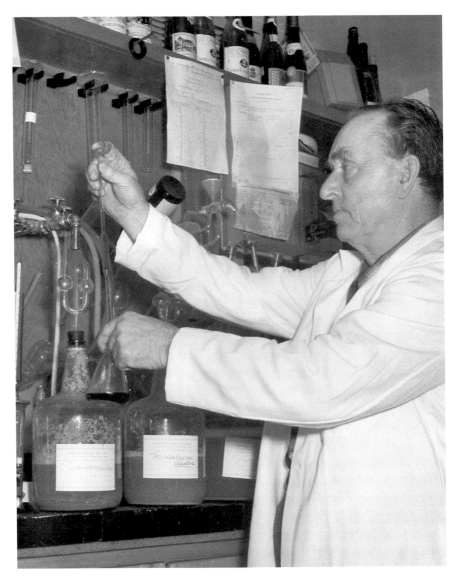

Dr. Frank in his lab at Vinifera Wine Cellars.

Konstantin's research in the station library revealed records dating back to 1902 experiments with *vinifera* at the Geneva station. Frank quoted from the *Station Bulletin* 432, no. 15 (April 1917), "*Vinifera* Grapes in New York," by R.D. Anthony and U.P. Hedrick: "Experimental Culture of the European grape was undertaken at this station in 1902 when cuttings or plants of 19 varieties were received.[49] In 1911, cuttings of more than 70 varieties were received and grafted...the results were very satisfactory, most of the plants were fruiting in 1913. By giving the vine winter protection and the usually grape spray, they have been kept in a healthy condition." In the same bulletin and in a different article, N.F. Hall wrote, "Failure is now preventable. Recent progress in grape culture proves that the old failures of European grapes were due to causes quite easily controlled; as we know, now, that many varieties of Vitis vinifera though not all, by any means, may be grown and ripened successfully in New York State."

Konstantin later wrote about these findings:

> *All of the other vinifera tested at this station are varieties growing in warm climates: table, raisin or sweet wine varieties from Russia, Conishons, Kalili, Roaski, from Egypt, muscat d'Alexandrie, from Mediterranean countries, southern France, Italy, Spain, Portugal and Greece and even Muscat Hamburg, and English variety which is mostly grown in the greenhouses in Belgium and England. Notwithstanding that these tested varieties are much less adapted to cold grape growing regions because of their freeze sensitiviness [sic] and need of longer growing seasons, at Geneva some of them survive since 1902 and 1911.[50]*

Why the scientists at Geneva had not appreciated their own successes cannot be known for certain, but it may be that they saw the *vinifera* growing at the station only as nursery stock necessary for their hybridization work and not as an experiment in growing *vinifera* itself. Still, with the evidence to the contrary growing on the station grounds for more than forty years, the official view of the station was to discourage interest in *vinifera* varieties as commercially viable.

It had not occurred to anyone that the presence of these vines would tend to refute the accepted wisdom. Konstantin must have been heartened when he read in U.P. Hedrick's *Manual of American Grape Growing* (1919), "At the New York Station, the European varieties are as vigorous and thrifty as American vines and are quite easily managed...Why may we not grow these grapes if we protect them from Phylloxera, fungi and cold?" Why not indeed?

This work by the station's own scientists, and by an eminent researcher such as Hedrick, had been completely lost or ignored by the 1950s, and what became the established wisdom in its place was exactly wrong. There may have been a number of factors behind this. First, the market was for large volumes of grapes for commercially produced juice and jelly and only secondarily for wine. The most prolific grapes for these purposes were the native varieties, particularly the *labrusca* grapes. If these grapes produced wine that required blending with California *vinifera*, or the additional sugar and alcohol to make them palatable, so be it. The American taste for wine at the time accepted sweet, alcoholic wine as the norm, and wine drinking in general had something of a distasteful reputation anyway. An argument could be made that even if *vinifera* could be grown, it could not compete with the yields of *labrusca* vines and would require more inputs and effort. Why grow an exotic grape that would be subject to damage or death from the predictably cold, wet winters of central New York? Why grow a grape that would produce fewer tons per acre for the sake of some claim to superior wine and value? What evidence suggested that the *vinifera* grapes, if brought to market, would command a price that would justify the extra expense and effort? What could compel a farmer to plant *vinifera* at such a risk when there was no market that would pay the premium price that would be needed for the grapes? The anticipated returns were dubious in the face of proven varieties and producers like Catawba, Concord and Niagara. The station was in the business of promoting successful agriculture, not spending resources promoting such a risky adventure.

"A State of Happy Mediocrity"

The market in the United States for fine wine was quite small at this time, and there was no "wine culture" that could be expected to eventually create demand. Wine drinkers might have been described as falling into one of two very general categories: snobs and skid row bums. There were many European immigrant families with a tradition of wine with meals and even winemaking, but these were not typical Americans of the 1950s—their wine production and consumption occurred outside the commercial marketplace. Prevailing wisdom at Geneva seemed to be that if wine was the goal of grape production, French-American hybrids, some developed right there in Geneva, were the obvious answer.

The simple truth was that since Prohibition, the demand for fine wine had been quite small; less than one gallon of wine per person was sold in the United States in the 1950s, and only 25 percent of that was table wine. For the most part, the American desire for fine wine was met by importing European wines and from California, where the conditions were right for wine grapes. Even French hybrids do not commonly reach full ripeness in the Finger Lakes in spite of being the preferred and recommended varieties. Because they are frequently picked early, when they are high in acid and low in sugar, they require chaptalization, or the process of adding sugar to bring up the alcohol level. New York wines were largely contrived beverages of fermented blends of grape juice, sugar and added alcohol, not to be confused with fine varietal wine. The results were of a character not held in high regard by most knowledgeable wine drinkers.

The accepted knowledge was that fine wines grow in places of fair climate, unlike New York. Dr. Frank's experience was a complete refutation of this accepted wisdom. He had grown *vinifera* in Ukraine, with winters as cold as if not colder than those of the Finger Lakes of New York. He had grown up in a tradition of fine wine being produced in a cold climate. He was unprepared for the reaction from other scientists to his claims for cold-climate *vinifera* and, one suspects, for the lack of interest in what he clearly knew would be superior wines. The fact was that no one was looking for anything better than what they already had. He described the wine industry in New York and the wine as being in a "state of happy mediocrity."[51]

In the frequent retelling of this part of his life, Konstantin referred to his job as "hoeing blueberries." Some doubt exists that this is strictly true, suggesting that Frank embellished the story to serve his own purposes and embarrass those in leadership in Geneva. It is, however, what he told his family and his friends at the time and over the years that followed.[52] Some associates who worked with him in the early years also acknowledge the story as true.[53] Some versions of his story have him working as a janitor, isolated and unable to communicate with his technical peers because he did not speak English, but these do not hold up under scrutiny. Karl Brase, his immediate supervisor, among others known to be at the station at that time were native German speakers and would have been able to converse with him. Sadly, the reality may have been worse. Konstantin could be understood, but the prevailing wisdom of the institution prevented him from being heard.

Perhaps the institutional inertia of Geneva and Cornell at the time did not allow for the possibility of big ideas that fell outside accepted knowledge, and no one was willing to buck the prevailing wisdom. The politics of

Cornell, and by extension the Geneva Experiment Station, at the time might have been summed up as "go along to get along." Grapes in New York were *labrusca* for juice and jelly. If grapes were needed for wine, there were the French hybrids or juice from California. Everyone knew that *Vitis vinifera* would not grow in New York State. The experiment at Bright's was just that—an experiment that would fail in the first cold winter. No one else at Geneva was willing to suggest otherwise and risk the internal political fallout that might result. Or perhaps it was as simple as the fact that *vinifera* was not on anyone's radar as a serious research subject. Whether he was actually hoeing blueberries or not, there is no doubt that Konstantin was relegated to the intellectual backwaters of the station.

Then, in the spring of 1953, Konstantin attended a seminar sponsored by the station that had invited scientists from around the world. It is likely that in the course of that seminar he met Charles Fournier, the president of Gold Seal Wines at that time. When Konstantin heard Fournier's French accent, he guessed that he was the winemaker from Gold Seal and he knew that he could be understood if he were to speak to him in French. He approached Fournier and told him that he could grow *vinifera* in the Finger Lakes. This immediately had Fournier's attention.

CHARLES FOURNIER AND GOLD SEAL

In Fournier, Frank found not only a sympathetic partner but one with whom he could articulate his ideas and arguments in French and get past the difficulties of his still developing command of English. He told Fournier of his success and his methods in Ukraine. He insisted that if it could be done there, it could be done here. Sometime in 1954, Fournier hired Dr. Frank to fill a new position at Gold Seal as director of vineyard research, the sole purpose of which was to develop a *vinifera* program for Gold Seal. Konstantin and Eugenia moved from Geneva to a rented house across the road from Keuka Lake and near the Gold Seal facilities. Frank started work on what would become his legacy: the successful commercial production of *vinifera* in the eastern United States.

The Gold Seal winery was established in 1865 as the Urbana Wine Company. It operated continuously in several locations until 1984, when the brand was sold. Gold Seal continues to operate as a brand, but the winery itself fell into disrepair over the years. The principal building of the winery

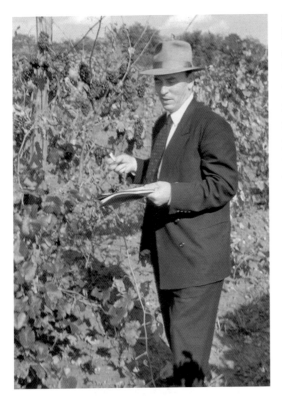

Dr. Frank in the vineyards at Gold Seal, 1953.

remains on the lake road. It is a spectacular stone and stucco building featuring a bell tower. There is a large veranda on the second floor that served as a space for outdoor wine tastings, parties and other events. In the early years, the lakefront was not as developed as it is today, and visitors would come by boat to events on the veranda, where they could partake of Gold Seal wine or champagne and enjoy the unobstructed view over Keuka Lake. The buildings have been purchased in recent years, and effort is being put into restoration.

Charles Fournier was born on June 15, 1902, in the Champagne region of France. His father was a judge but had decided early on that Charles should follow in the steps of his uncle and become a winemaker. Charles became a winemaker for the famous Widow Clicquot's Veuve Clicquot Ponsardin House of Champagne at the age of twenty-five and production manager only three years later. Meanwhile, the wine industry in the United States was in a shambles. Years of Prohibition had resulted in a loss of experience and expertise in winemaking. Many winemakers looked abroad for talented artisans who could be lured away. These circumstances are what brought Andres de Chaunac, Charles Fournier and Andre Tchelistcheff from Europe to the United States and Canada. Others, including Konstantin Frank, Mike Ggrich and Hermann Weimer, would follow.

After several concerted efforts beginning in 1930, the owners of the Urbana Wine Company were finally able to recruit Fournier to come to the Finger Lakes and join the company, later called Gold Seal, as winemaker and production manager. He was tasked with improving the quality of the wine to at least pre-Prohibition levels. He was unprepared for what he found when he arrived in the Finger Lakes. "I had no idea of the climate or the grapes I would have to work with." He told a reporter later, "It was a sultry 100 degrees Fahrenheit in the shade when I arrived in New York. Then I tasted Concord, Catawba, Elvira and Isabelle wine, which to say the least gave me a shock. The winter that followed gave me a third shock! But as I had signed a one year contract, I stuck it out."[54]

Fournier did a masterful job getting the winery up and running again using the French-American hybrids and other varieties commonly grown for wine in New York and juice from California. He hired others with expertise in winemaking, including Alexander Brailow, the Russian who had invited Konstantin to live in his home when he first arrived. After some experimentation, Fournier found he could produce traditional champagne flavors using hybrid and native grapes grown in the right soils. In short order, Gold Seal was producing excellent sparkling wine once again. In 1950, a Gold Seal sparkling wine won the only gold medal in its category at the California State Fair. The embarrassed response from the California wineries was to close future competitions to out-of-state wineries. Although Fournier was successful with his formulations of natives and hybrids, he retained his interest, and hope, to one day make wine from *vinifera* again.

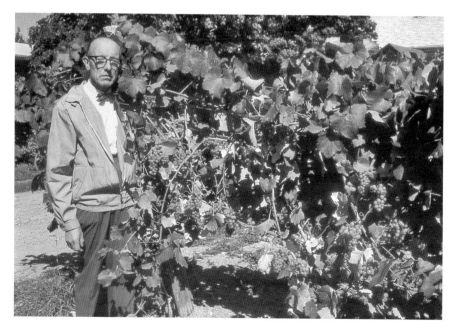

Charles Fournier.

Coming from the cool Champagne region of France, Fournier was familiar with the idea of microclimates and the importance of site selection for a winery and vineyards. As he became familiar with the area surrounding his new home, he began to evaluate the land for appropriate sites for vineyards and look seriously at the French hybrid varieties being promoted as alternative wine grapes in the eastern United States. He read Philip Wagner's book and articles and wrote to Wagner about supplying cuttings. At that time, Wagner had only recently started his nursery and was selling French-American hybrids. Fournier established a research effort to find the best hybrids—French or American—that had the best combination of hardiness, disease resistance and flavor. Philip Wagner became a close friend and trusted source of information and cuttings. Both Wagner and Fournier lamented the poor prospects for growing *vinifera* in the eastern United States. When Fournier met Dr. Frank, his interest in *vinifera* was renewed, and his passion for the possibilities rekindled.

Frank and Fournier understood that the keys to success for *vinifera* in the Finger Lakes lie in finding the right varieties and the right environments in which to plant them. The right microclimates would take advantage of the lake effect air drainage and optimize the mediating effects of the climate by virtue of the correct proximity to the water. Within the general lake effect phenomenon were microclimates where the benefits of the lake effect were enhanced by virtue of soil quality and site topography and aspect. In addition to identifying the best microclimates, finding the right rootstocks was critical. To make a successful graft of the rootstock and the scion, a section of the desired fruiting plant is carefully joined so that the cambium (the vascular layer of plant tissues immediately under the bark) of the rootstock and the scion match with each other. It is the contact between the cambium of the scion and the cambium of the rootstock that makes the graft function. The roots and the vine are able to exchange fluids via the healed vascular system and grow as a single plant.

Using this technique, a given variety of grape's susceptibility to phylloxera or frozen soils can be offset by using rootstocks resistant to those problems. All grafts are not equal, though, so finding the best match between rootstock variety and scion variety was a critical aspect of Konstantin's work. More than just cold hardiness, the rootstocks had to also match well with the variety. Field trials were necessary to be sure that the root/scion matches produced a desirable vine, as well as desirable fruit. It was important, in Fournier's words, to "avoid excess of vigor." He believed that excessively large canes would freeze more readily and so vines that were too vigorous would be more likely to suffer damage from the cold winters. Also, root/scion combinations that produced too much fruit could weaken canes, and this reduces their ability to resist the effects of cold. For nearly five years, Fournier and Frank traveled around the northeastern United States and southeastern Canada, visiting places where they might find rootstocks to use in their experiments.

The image of the debonair Fournier and the rumpled Frank driving around the northeastern United States and southeastern Canada in Fournier's Alfa Romeo, in search of native rootstocks on which to build the *vinifera*, the possibilities gleaming in their eyes, is difficult to resist. Eventually, they collected rootstocks from all over the region and some from as far away as Texas. In a small monastery vineyard in Joliette, Quebec, they visited a priest, I.A. Savinac, who had been growing more than one hundred varieties of *vinifera* without any winter protection for fifteen years. Even though the short 120-day growing season produced fruit only one year in three, the vines survived the Canadian winters.[55] They collected cuttings from the vines that were the most productive, and eventually they had a sufficient number of rootstocks to begin their work. Along the miles and hours on the road, sharing their visions of the possibilities, they became fast and lifelong friends, with several shared interests.

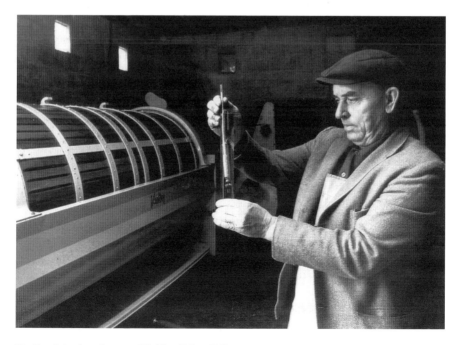

Dr. Frank in the winery at Vinifera Wine Cellars.

To be successful with *vinifera*, Dr. Frank understood that he had to overcome or mitigate a number of factors: the threat of phylloxera to the *vinifera* varieties, the fungal diseases that are native to North America and finally the climate. The solution to the phylloxera problem was well established. Interestingly, Dr. Frank had been involved with experiments addressing the phylloxera problem while working in Europe and Ukraine, and successful strategies had been developed. Addressing the fungi problem would be an ongoing issue for vineyard managers, but one that could be managed. Fungicides already developed and under development helped manage the fungus attacks; developing the appropriate strategies for their use was the focus of vineyard managers and scientists at the experiment station. The climate was the only remaining obstacle to growing the noble varieties of wine in the eastern United States. His experience on the former Troubetskoy estate turned agricultural experiment station had included solving these very problems.

The Troubetskoy estate had a similar, if not actually colder, climate compared to central New York. At Troubetskoy's vineyards, the sloping land and the moderating effect of the river resulted in a microclimate in which the *vinifera* vines could grow. The legend is that Catherine the Great gave the land to a prince. In an effort to make the fallow land productive, he invited two monks—one from France and one from Germany—for the purpose of establishing a huge vineyard nine miles long and four miles wide situated along the slopes above the Dnieper River. The monks planted the *vinifera* varieties of their respective homelands. Two hundred years later, the vineyard was destroyed by phylloxera at about the same time as that of Damian Frank.

When Konstantin was assigned the task of managing the estate for the Soviet government, his job was largely to reestablish the vineyards that had been destroyed in the revolution and the deprivation that followed. He understood that to do so he would have to use phylloxera-resistant rootstocks, but he would also have to protect the graft from the effects of the cold Russian winters. Much of his work was involved in finding first the best rootstocks and then the most effective cultural methods to ensure their survival and productivity. Among the innovations he developed was a plow that would turn the earth in the fall to cover the graft and uncover it again in the spring. He also invented a special deep-cutting plow that would break up the soil for newly planted vineyards.

He had proven his methods once. Now in America, relying on that experience, Dr. Frank selected land for vineyards to take the greatest advantage of the lake effect. He would employ the same techniques that had worked so well at home. From the beginning of his work, he welcomed people interested in growing grapes and making wine. He understood that if his ideas were to be successful, the information had to spread beyond Gold Seal, and he set about spreading the word to anyone who was interested. He remained, in a sense, a teacher, but a teacher who brooked no dissent or disagreement from his students or colleagues.

The move to Gold Seal allowed Konstantin and Eugenia to move into a house owned by the company. The house was situated near the Gold Seal facility on the shores of Keuka Lake. In the evenings after work, the Franks could go swimming or fish in the lake across the road from their house. Eugenia was pleased that she could once again have a small garden, and the village of Hammondsport was just down the road. Konstantin reveled in the work before him at Gold Seal. He was always focused on the task before him, with little care or concern for personal appearances. He is often remembered as wearing threadbare suits and clothing, not caring or unaware of their condition or not willing to spend the money to replace them. Fournier, on the other hand, is always remembered as urbane and well dressed. Acquaintances from this time remember Konstantin as affable but demanding when it came to his work. Eugenia is most often remembered as quiet and supportive but very determined in her own way.

Over the next seven years, Konstantin would oversee the propagation of grafts combining *vinifera* with more than sixty different rootstocks, ranging from old rootstocks developed from American native varieties in Europe to varieties collected by Fournier and Frank in Quebec and the woods around Keuka Lake. The scion wood was acquired from the University of California–Davis, from Bright's Wine Cellars in Canada and from the New York Experiment Station at Geneva. In addition, they worked closely with the United States Department of Agriculture, Agricultural Research Division in Beltsville, Maryland, to test thirty different clones of Riesling, Gewurztraminer and Muscat Ottonel. Over these years, Konstantin expanded the research plots by about fifteen acres per year.[56]

Another of the challenges Konstantin faced was the extraordinary number of soil types to be found over relatively short distances in the Finger Lakes. In Ukraine, soils were more homogenous. In an article he published, he noted, "In my experience I have never met such enormous changing of soil types on such a very small area. In a row of 70 vines, the soil changed 7 times."[57] He worked closely with local officials from the Soil Conservation Agency, and with their help, he produced detailed maps of the soils in the experimental vineyards.[58] This variability affected the research program significantly since the research had to consider not only the scion-rootstock combination but also how that combination worked in different soil types. Konstantin wrote, "It is normal to expect that these very different types of soil will in different degrees influence the adaptability of the rootstock. Therefore on this experimental plot we have noted, as we suspected, different vigor, different adaptability, different freeze resistance and different freeze damage and naturally different productivity of grape varieties tested on this experimental plot."[59] This required the soils in the experiment plots to be closely mapped and then planting plans laid out so that the same grafts would be planted across different soils. Then, close recordkeeping would be done to measure variance in the vigor of growth, productivity, blossom time, the time fruit ripened, leaf coloring, the time the leaves fell, the degree of wood ripening, freeze resistance and so on. Groups of like vines on like soils would be harvested together, weighed, analyzed and made into wine in small batches for comparison. This exhaustive approach would ultimately yield the best combinations of wood and root for specific soil types.

Charles Fournier wrote an article in 1961 in which he recalled the story of their success:

> *After five years and hundreds of thousands of grafts, a list of successful combinations was arrived at, and in the fall of 1957 our first plantings of Johannisberger Riesling and Pinot Chardonnay produced grapes that had more than 23% sugar at the beginning of October plus an acidity high enough for very good balance. During the winter of 1956–57, the region was struck by one of the cold spells which hit the northeast every 5 to 7 years. For three nights the temperature dropped to 10 to 25 below zero on the slopes of the lake…. The Vinifera in most instances came out as well as the most resistant hybrids, and less than 10% of the buds were hurt. I did not need to be convinced further and planting was then started commercially as fast as we could get enough rootstock in our nursery.*[60]

The winter long predicted by critics had occurred, and the *vinifera* survived, as Konstantin said it would. Under Fournier's direction, Gold Seal planted seventy acres of *vinifera* vines the next year.

This research program was not conducted in isolation. As already noted, the USDA, Cornell University and the experiment station at Geneva were all engaged in aspects of the research program, but other winemakers, growers and scientists were also on site for frequent visits to

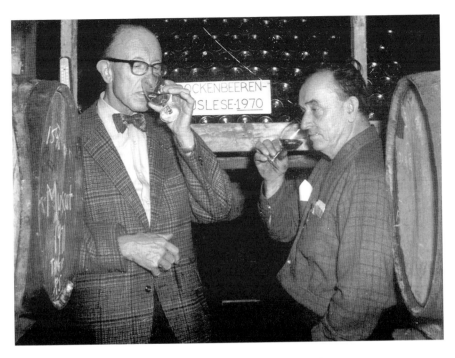

Charles Fournier and Dr. Frank in the cellar at Vinifera Wine Cellars.

the Gold Seal research plots. Dr. Frank was forthcoming with his results—good and bad, he shared them all. By the late 1950s, there was a buzz of interest over what Dr. Konstantin Frank was doing at Gold Seal. Letters of congratulations and appreciation were sent to Fournier and Dr. Frank from notable people in the wine industry and in the research community. The position at Gold Seal allowed Konstantin and Eugenia to travel around the United States to visit winemakers and wineries in California, Virginia and places in between. He used these visits to establish relationships with people all over the country. Wine writers began to ask for information and interviews. Konstantin invited them all to see what he was doing. Pennsylvania State University, Cornell University, various branches within the USDA, county agents, farmers and many others sent individuals or delegations to see the remarkable results of the field research being done at Gold Seal. Charles Fournier invited his friend Philip Wagner to visit the vineyards and taste the wine. Wagner wrote to Fournier, "Dr. Frank's work so far is very impressive and my interest in following the vinifera much increased. Both of the wines were very good. But it is the Cabernet that really catches my eye and arouses my hope."[61]

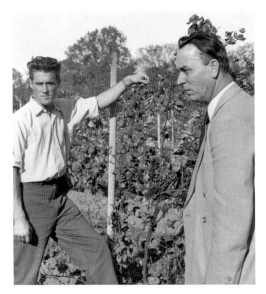

Darmon Gleason and Dr. Frank in the Gold Seal vineyards.

With his growing success, Frank began to insist that Gold Seal remove all of its French hybrids and replace them with *vinifera*. The owners and management of Gold Seal were predictably reluctant to follow this advice. While Konstantin Frank was the director of research, the head winemaker at Gold Seal was Alexander Brailow, and while he acknowledged the success and promise of *vinifera*, he was reluctant to move away from the blends and grape varieties that were the core of Gold Seal's current success. Brailow was not alone. Most people were cautious about the success of the *vinifera* and still considered it little more than a promising research experiment. The general line of thought was that it was, at best, a risky proposition and that a cold winter would end it all. All of the previous attempts in growing *vinifera* in the East pointed to the ultimate failure of any attempt at commercial levels of production. Charles Fournier, however, saw the potential for *vinifera*. "There is a tremendous future for *vinifera* in the eastern United States," he said. "They make wines with more flavor than their counterparts in California."[62] Some years later, Fournier would say, "I had been trying to grow hybrids since the 1930s and had some success but I knew hybrids were not the answer. I knew they would never make big wines. I thought Dr. Frank could bring us true *vinifera*."[63] Even Fournier, however, could not agree to a total rapid conversion from the natives and French hybrids; the business implications were too great. The answer was no, but for Dr. Frank, the word *no* didn't mean "no." It meant "try harder."[64]

Konstantin tried harder, but with only nominal success. He also pushed for more and more acreage to be used for research and experiments. Eventually, managers at Gold Seal began to balk at the scale of the research program and the resources it was consuming. Acreage dedicated to research projects could not produce any wine to sell, and they were in the business of selling wine.

Former Gold Seal workers can remember heated discussions in German or Russian between Brailow and Frank over the *vinifera* question.[65]

In 1957, Konstantin became a proud and patriotic U.S. citizen, and one year later, he purchased 118 acres for $6,000 on the western shore of Keuka Lake. He understood that the fairly complex science of matching rootstocks and scions needed to be matched also to soils and an environment conducive to the vines' growth. Site selection was the first decision so critical to the success of his venture. Eugenia once recalled to her daughter Lena that when they first visited the site of the farm that would eventually become his winery, the existing house and buildings were falling down and the fields had become overgrown and scrubby, but Konstantin seemed to not see that as he bent down, fingered a handful of earth and said to her with a smile, "Good soil."[66] At the age of fifty-nine, he began to plant *vinifera* with weekend and evening help from volunteers from Gold Seal and even a few from the Geneva Experiment Station.[67] He intentionally extended the Gold Seal research program onto his own land, using his own acreage to supplement that of Gold Seal. He not only planned to demonstrate that he could grow *vinifera*, but he also expected from the very beginning to attract and help others do the same.

In addition to his research plantings, he began to plant some vines to be used for commercial wine production and started his own nursery—creating, in every practical sense, his own personal experiment station. He would produce and sell wine primarily to show the quality of the *vinifera* grapes

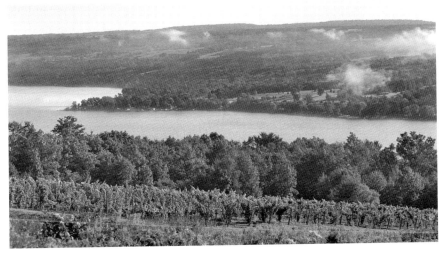

A view of the vineyards and Keuka Lake from the Vinifera Wine Cellars.

but also to fund his experiments. He foresaw a time when *vinifera* would be grown "in 20 or 30 states" outside California, and he saw a role for himself in helping the transition along.[68] He wrote in 1973, "My principles and my philosophy have always been growing and teaching how to grow the best grape varieties and make the best wine." With the help of Eugenia; his son-in-law, Walter Volz; and frequent weekend help from his son, Willy Frank, he began to grow what would eventually become more than sixty varieties of *vinifera* grapes on his farm. With the help of former assistants from Gold Seal like Darmon Gleason, Konstantin and Eugenia made thousands more grafts as he searched for the best possible root/scion match for each variety, eventually identifying the combinations that produced the hardiest and most productive vines.

He would eagerly share his knowledge and the results of his experiments and research with anyone who would ask. He provided opportunities for them to work with him and learn what he knew and was discovering. He ran an informal internship program for many years, letting interested folks work a season or a harvest alongside Walter Volz and the crews. These were his students; he called them his "cooperators" and encouraged them to start their own ventures. Among his cooperators who spent time with him and went on to their own successes were Douglas Moorhead (Presque Isle Wine Cellars, Pennsylvania), Arnulf Esterer (Markko Vineyards, Ohio), Hamilton Mowbray (Montbray Cellars, Maryland), Elizabeth Furness (Piedmont Vineyards, Virginia) and George Matheson (Chicama Vineyards, Massachusetts), among others. He had the knack of meeting the right people, promoting his ideas and having his cooperators promote them, too.

The phylloxera problem had long since been solved, and, in Frank's view, so had the concern with climate. He would tell anyone who would listen that he had grown *vinifera* in Ukraine, where in winter "it was so cold your spit would freeze before it hit the ground." He did not understand why Americans would settle for inferior wine, and in his view, anything but wine made from *vinifera* would be inferior. He told a local newspaper reporter in 1982, "*Vitis vinifera* has ten thousand species but only ten or twelve of ten thousand are really excellent. I introduce them and I do promote them to be grown in all States of the USA."

The field trials at Gold Seal were successfully demonstrating the viability of *vinifera* in the Finger Lakes, and Konstantin continued to insist that more effort be put into research and more production be given over to *vinifera*.[69] The arguments between Konstantin and Alexander Brailow grew more frequent and heated. Konstantin could not understand the reluctance to abandon what he knew to be obviously inferior grapes in favor of the noble varieties. In the face of continued resistance to his proposals from the Gold Seal leadership, he become more focused on working his own land and expanding the research with help from family, off-duty Gold Seal employees and friends, even as he continued to manage Gold Seal's research effort. New field trials along the shore of Lake Erie thrived and had opened yet another region for *vinifera* production; new success fueled his push for more acreage to be converted from French hybrids.

As the success with *vinifera* became better known, Konstantin worked with interested growers and oversaw plantings along Lake Erie in Pennsylvania. He was also providing advice and cuttings to growers on Long Island. At every turn, his efforts were paying off and demonstrating that *vinifera* could be grown on a commercial scale in the Northeast. Still, the managers at Gold Seal remained unsure of the viability of the European vines and were reluctant to commit more resources, as they had already planted more than seventy acres with *vinifera* at some cost and risk. To risk more might jeopardize the business of sweet and fortified wines, which were the most profitable. The business model using hybrid and native varieties (adding some juice from California as well as sugar and alcohol as needed) was profitable, and from

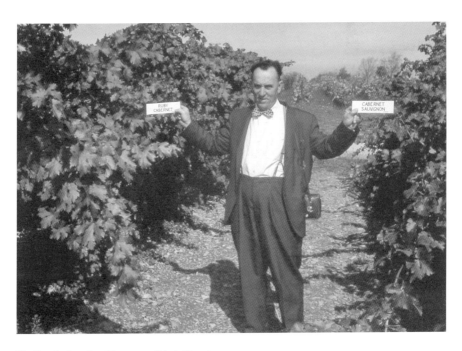

Dr. Frank showing his successful *vinifera* vines.

their view, there was nothing to suggest a change. If the investment in *vinifera* paid off, they would respond accordingly, but the perceived risks and costs of converting even larger vineyards to *vinifera* without some demonstrable market were just too high. Even his old friend Charles Fournier understood the reluctance to move as quickly as Konstantin urged.

The first releases from Gold Seal's *vinifera* were met with much acclaim. Charles Fournier's dream of making fine table wine in New York had come to fruition. Konstantin's own Vinifera Wine Cellars were still a few years in the future, but the clouds of disagreement with the Geneva Experiment Station were still gathering and would continue to do so for more than two decades. Still, it might have been some consolation that some there had already started to appreciate his work. In 1959, Arthur Heiniche of the New York State Department of Agriculture wrote to Dr. Frank, "The work you are doing shows promise of being very valuable, not only to Gold Seal Vineyards, but to the New York grape industry as a whole."

Part III

"ONLY EXCELLENT"

VINIFERA WINE CELLARS

In 1961, Konstantin retired from Gold Seal. Some said that the acrimony that existed as a result of his insistence on abandoning French hybrids in favor of *vinifera* had reached a point that he was fired while Fournier was away on business and not available to shield him. Although possible, most recall that the decision was entirely Konstantin's. It may be that he had his fill of trying to convince others of his vision and was finally able to strike off on his own. It is more likely that he was ready to devote himself to his mission, for that is what it had become, to promote *vinifera* and demonstrate its viability and superiority over other varieties of grapes grown for wine. He had already purchased a farm and built a house. Many acres of vineyards were already planted; it is likely that it was just time to make the move.

As the owner of his own enterprise, he would plant only *vinifera*, he would produce "only excellent" wine and he would convince the naysayers. The name of the new business left no doubt as to his intentions; the company letterhead would have cleared up any confusion. It read, "Dr. Konstantin Frank and Sons—Experimental Nursery, Vineyards, and Vinifera Wine Cellars, European Grape Varieties and European Estate Bottled Wine." The purpose of the Vinifera Wine Cellars would be to build on his work at Gold Seal, to demonstrate conclusively that *vinifera* could be successfully grown on a commercial scale in the Finger Lakes and to share his knowledge with as

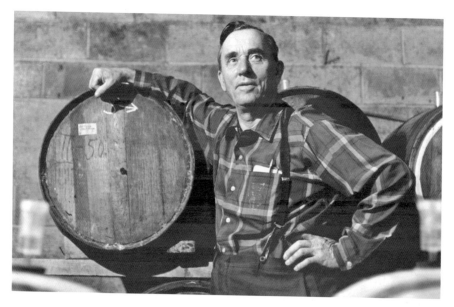

Dr. Frank in the winery barrel room.

many people as would listen. He also understood that for fine winemaking to succeed, both the number of wine enthusiasts and the market would have to grow. He believed that if more Americans had some understanding and access to good wine, they would drink it. So, as his success in the vineyards was established, his mission expanded to include promoting a wine culture such as he had known in Europe and Russia. From the outset, he envisioned Vinifera Wine Cellars as more of a privately run experiment station than a strictly commercial winery. He believed that through demonstration and education he would contribute to the nascent American wine culture. The following year, in 1962, he released the first vintage from the Vinifera Wine Cellars. He was sixty-three years old, and he had been in the United States for just eleven years.

The winery buildings had been started shortly after Konstantin had purchased the property, and Konstantin and Eugenia built a new house on the site of the dilapidated house that was there when they bought the land. The new house was made entirely of brick, with a kitchen large enough to serve meals to a growing family that now included grandchildren. A breezeway was constructed to enjoy the shade and capture the cooling summer breeze. These two features of the house quickly became the center of activity. In the years to come, many visitors to the winery would enjoy glasses of wine, listening to Konstantin's stories and ideas. Among the earliest efforts Konstantin undertook was to have his wine accepted for use in the sacraments of the church. Always a devout Catholic, Konstantin was pleased and proud when he received word that his wine was approved to be used as sacramental wine by the bishop of the Diocese of Rochester, New York.

When they finally moved out of the house rented from Gold Seal on Lower Lake Road, Eugenia planted a large garden for flowers and vegetables. Konstantin established bee colonies and built a coop for chickens. The bees he kept were for pollination, honey and for treatment of his arthritis—he would catch bees and hold them up to his back and knees to be stung. Eugenia never learned to drive, so living up on the hill, away from any neighbors, was isolating. She continued to be active in the church, especially with the children's choir, but every trip to Hammondsport required being driven by Konstantin, a skill he never mastered. So, every trip contained the promise of some adventure. Konstantin tended to drive in the middle of the narrow country roads and not readily give way to oncoming traffic. Fortunately, there was little traffic, and his neighbors apparently learned to watch for him coming.

The relationship between Konstantin and Eugenia was very private. Like her husband, she was a product of being brought up in the Old World and accepted her life and role as keeper of the home, cook and mother. While Konstantin sought to prove his ideas, to gain attention and publicity, she remained anchored in the background and at home. She worked side by side with him, grafting and planting vines, pruning and harvesting, and she was present when bottling was done; when the work was done, she would feed the workers. While she said little, Konstantin listened closely to what she said—a word or a look from Mama was usually enough. The experience of loss and reestablishing their lives on several occasions had taught all of them to be frugal and to appreciate what they had. Once asked if she would like to learn to drive so she could get around herself, go places and see friends, Eugenia said simply, "It is better to stay home. Save money."[70] The Franks did travel, though. During some of the New York winters, they continued to travel to different wine regions in the United States, most notably Sonoma Valley in California—where they stayed with friends from Germany—but also wineries in Virginia and elsewhere.

Like Eugenia, Konstantin was a product of his experience. From his privileged childhood, through the disruption and loss of revolution, war and the mistrust born of years under Soviet rule, he had learned to measure trust carefully and to rely largely on himself and family. His experience with bureaucracies, first in the Soviet Union and more recently with the experiment station and Gold Seal, had left him with little confidence or faith in such institutions. He understood that to succeed one had to be resolute and assertive. His experience at Gold Seal had taught him something about America, too.

During the years of the *vinifera* experiment at Gold Seal, Fournier and Frank had invited scientists, winemakers, public officials and others to come and visit the vineyards to see for themselves the *vinifera* growing and flourishing year after year. These visitors included some skeptics, of course, but also at least as many enthusiastic supporters. Konstantin learned the value of having a network of such supporters to spread the news and to draw the interest of important people. He knew to manage and cultivate his contacts in earnest. He built on early relationships made possible by reputation and the business gravitas of Gold Seal and Fournier and made them his own as he set out to promote *vinifera*. If he did not already know the value of publicity, he quickly learned. He established longstanding relationships with officials from the federal and state departments of agriculture; with elected officials, businesspeople and college professors; and with wine writers. Konstantin recognized the value of powerful and influential friends, and he unabashedly sought out and encouraged such relationships. As the news of his successes at Gold Seal and then at the Vinifera Wine Cellars spread, more wine enthusiasts sought out Dr. Frank.

He learned and mastered the art of self-promotion. If he spied a likely ally, or an attractive woman, visiting his operation, he would stop what he was doing to sit on his porch and regale his visitor with his ideas. He would invite them into the vineyards to witness the vigor and abundance of the *vinifera* growing there. Professionals, politicians, professors, businesspeople and not a few attractive ladies would be invited to enjoy some wine, and as they sipped, he would freely share his knowledge and opinions. Among his network of enthusiasts were many who became his students—or, as he referred

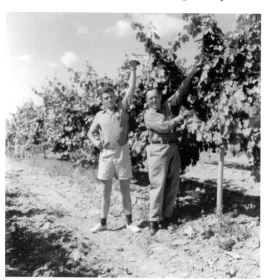

Walter Volz and Dr. Frank in the vineyard.

to them, his "cooperators"—who would take what they learned and begin their own vineyards. He was not shy about promoting his views and his passion, and he did not hesitate to ask others to help him in this effort; and yet, he did not accept criticism lightly and frequently became combative with critics and naysayers. This, coupled with his vigorous promotion of his ideas, earned him some enmity among other growers and winemakers. Still, Konstantin seemed to understand the powerful combination of a good idea and the value of a well-connected network, and he continued to push against the status quo.

Frank and Sons

Along with that resolve to follow his own passion, Konstantin remained dedicated to his family. He envisioned the farm as a family operation—he longed to have all of his children working and living together on the land above Keuka Lake, just as his father's family had lived when he was a boy. He chose to name his new business Dr. Konstantin Frank and Sons' Vinifera Wine Cellars. Although he had only one son, he hoped to have his sons-in-law join the family business. Being of an old-school mindset, he apparently did not consider his daughters as prospective partners, but he held on to the hope and the dream that his children and their families would join him in the business. He hoped to re-create the family compound—the life spent working and living together that he recalled from the Ukraine.

He invited his children and their spouses to come and join him in the Finger Lakes, work beside him building the new business and share in his vision. His children, however, had been busy establishing their own lives. His youngest daughter, Lena Schelling, declined his invitation, electing to stay in the life she was enjoying in Catskill, New York, where her husband, Ed Schelling, owned a successful insurance agency.[71] Willy expressed interest but was wary of joining the business without a clear understanding of his role; without such an understanding, he declined.[72] Willy's career was going well, and eventually he became a successful manufacturer's representative for photographic equipment. His success enabled Margrit and him to travel extensively, and they enjoyed the society of good friends and a good life in Valley Stream on Long Island. Willy also understood that the business and the vision were his father's and that all decisions would be made and direction given by Konstantin. There would be one leader, there

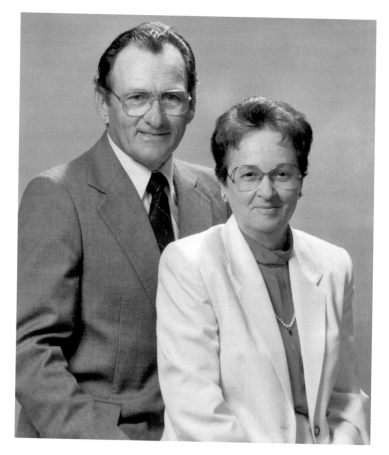

Walter and Hilda Volz.

would be one vision and there would be only one way—Konstantin's way. Willy was reluctant to join the business and abandon his success in New York City without the capacity to fully participate in running the business.

Only Konstantin's daughter Hilda and her husband, Walter Volz, agreed to join him and to work at the winery. Walter had grown up in Bavaria and, like Konstantin, was an avid fisherman and hunter; life in the Finger Lakes offered access to the countryside where these pleasures could be pursued. The move meant that Walter would have to leave a good job as a machinist in New Jersey and relocate his wife and their small children to the Finger Lakes for the uncertainty of a startup business. Although Walter knew little about grapes or winemaking, he felt that he would be learning directly from the expert. If things should go badly, he was still only twenty-eight years old, with time to recover and start over. Walter and Hilda accepted the invitation in part for the opportunity to be in on the business from the beginning but also with the understanding that Willy and Margrit would be joining them.[73] Walter knew Konstantin and expected that working for his father-in-law would be a demanding and likely thankless undertaking, but if Willy were there to share the burden, he believed it could be a good life. Together they could make working for "Papa" tolerable. As it turned out, Willy would not come for many years; meanwhile, Walter was subjected to Dr. Frank's demanding regimen of work. If Dr. Frank wanted to work late, as he often did, Walter was expected to work late as well. There were few days or weekends off and fewer vacations except by working alongside his father-in-law.[74]

Over time, Walter learned and became an expert vineyard manager, earning the respect of the neighboring growers, vineyard managers and the people who made up much of the seasonal labor on which the vineyard depended. Walter Volz worked side by side with Dr. Frank for the next twenty-five years, learning everything the doctor could offer about growing grapes and managing vineyards. He would labor always under the demanding shadow of his father-in-law, who was clearly the mind behind the operations. However, for many people who worked in the vineyards, Walter Volz became the heart and soul of the vineyards at Vinifera Wine Cellars. Walter was there every day—in the field, under the sun, in the cold with the workers, carrying out Konstantin's vision. Between the two of them, they created remarkable vineyards and a collection of *vinifera* grapes. Andre Tchelistcheff, the modern-day father of California wine, would one day tell winemakers in California to visit Vinifera Wine Cellars on their travels east "just to see the vineyards."[75]

Willy would not join the business full time for more than twenty years but would come up frequently from Long Island to work on projects or the harvest. His name, however, appeared on the business letterhead from the beginning. In spite of his presence on the ground and daily contribution, Walter's name was never added to the letterhead. For Konstantin, the business was Dr. Konstantin Frank and Sons—that should be enough. Even at a distance, Willy and Konstantin maintained a fractious relationship at best. Konstantin was as demanding and unreasonable with Walter and Willy as he was with his critics. When Willy would come up on weekends, he and his father would invariably argue. Whether it was paperwork, construction issues, marketing and sales, wine tasting or finance, an argument would develop over something. Dr. Frank wanted his son to join the business to

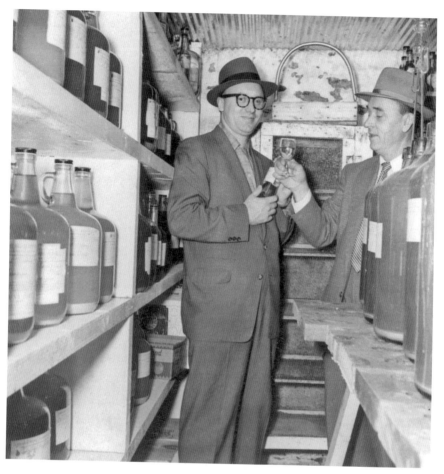

Willy Frank and Dr. Frank with samples of wine.

do marketing and sales, but at the same time, he distrusted Willy's business background. He felt that Willy would only understand profits and business and would not care about the quality of the vineyards and the *vinifera* mission as he did. For his part, Willy knew that without a clearly spelled-out arrangement, he would never have any authority to make decisions or run the business *as* a business, so he did not join Walter. In the meantime, Walter Volz worked in the vineyards and learned the cycle of growth and harvest and the vineyard techniques required by Konstantin and saw the results of the work in the vineyard as it moved from field to bottle to glass. Where Willy confronted his father, Walter sought accommodation and a peaceful day-to-day relationship with his father-in-law.

Konstantin was committed to demonstrating his findings on a grand scale, and so, with the continued help of some Gold Seal employees on weekends and the occasional loan of some equipment, he and Walter planted many varieties of *Vitis vinifera*. This was an extension of his experimentation and development work that he had begun at Gold Seal. He wanted to grow as many varieties of *vinifera* as he could to learn and demonstrate which varieties grew best. At one time, as many as sixty varieties or more of *vinifera* were grown on his property. The number alone can be misleading, though. Some of these varieties were never more than twenty or thirty vines, some perhaps as few as four vines—enough to satisfy the interests of research,

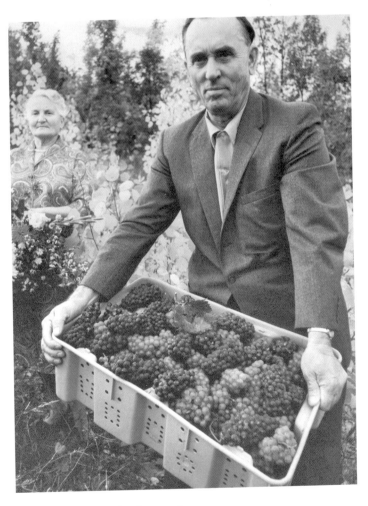

Eugenia and Dr. Frank at harvest time.

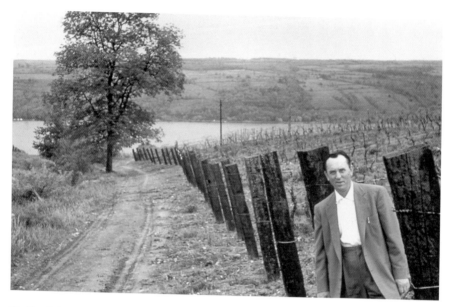

Dr. Frank in the vineyards at Vinifera Wine Cellars.

though.[76] His primary focus for the enterprise was as an experiment station, so he kept detailed records on each group of vines. He collected, counted and weighed the production of particular individual vines as part of the scion/stock evaluation process.

Grapes were harvested by hand and processed in limited batches, each a separate wine that would be tested, tasted and evaluated. Then, all of the small batches, some from only a few vines and others a row or two, would be combined and bottled for sale. In some cases, the entire crop of a variety might make less than ten gallons of wine. It was Walter's job to manage this process in the field and in the harvest. For example, when it was time to harvest the Riesling, it was not a single harvest, per se, but rather many small harvests of individual rows, or portions of rows, that required tracking from the vineyard through the crush and all the way through the winemaking process. Once the wine was ready, tasted and evaluated, then all of these small harvests and unique wines were blended together for bottling and sale. The focus was on the science, but producing and selling wine was necessary to fund the research underway at the Vinifera Wine Cellars. In the end, of course, excellent wine would be the most convincing proof of Dr. Frank's conviction.

A Missionary's Zeal

Konstantin understood that this sort of experimentation was mostly of interest only to other scientists and growers and that the wine itself was the best means of attracting a wider audience. The market for his ideas was very limited, and in the end, all of the experimentation would come down to what was in the glass. In the 1960s, commercial distribution in New York could only be done through the distributor system or directly by a winery owner. Compared to the large wine companies, Vinifera Wine Cellars was too small to interest most distributors and too small to have a major marketing presence, so sales and marketing directly to buyers was necessary. Konstantin took every opportunity to talk about his ideas as much as his wine; he would travel throughout the eastern United States to conduct wine tastings for clubs, social organizations and restaurant patrons. He would contact those folks who sat in his breezeway and his cooperators and offer to do wine tastings for their local clubs or organizations.

Since there was only a very small market for eastern table wines, he would travel and meet with interested people to create interest in his wine but also to educate his audience so they could learn about wine. He quickly capitalized on the value of free publicity and marketing from the press and invited reporters and wine writers to visit the Vinifera Wine Cellars. These articles drew the attention of knowledgeable people in the wine industry and academia. Even in the early 1960s, he started to receive visitors from around the United States and Europe. Konstantin loved nothing more than to meet these visitors and preside over tastings and tell them his story. Although his early wines received critical attention and approval, the level of production at the Vinifera Wine Cellars remained too small to attract large distributors or realize the cost to hire salespeople. So, typical of Konstantin, if it was to be done, he was the one to do it. His mission was first to educate and then to sell. His tastings were unusual because he did not stand behind a table and describe each wine as he poured. Rather, he delivered a full-blown lecture on wine, grapes and winemaking before any wine was poured. He was bent on serving his wine to an informed consumer and set about informing them at every tasting.

As the tastings grew more frequent, his lecture became more polished and entertaining, so people attending the tastings remembered Konstantin as much as they remembered the wine—perhaps more so. Some of them would subsequently travel to Keuka Lake to visit him at the winery, and many of them spread his word to their interested friends; over time, he developed a loyal and enthusiastic following that continues to this day. His schedule was demanding. These were the days before the completion of major highway routes, and travel from Keuka Lake meant driving, a task at which Konstantin was not very proficient. So, over the years, several good friends volunteered to drive him and his wine from tasting to tasting, with cars loaded down with cases of wine. Although he was nearly seventy years old at the time, he would continue this pace, traveling widely throughout the eastern United States for another ten years.

While Konstantin was on the road, selling wine and the good life and building his brand and his vineyards, the officials at the agricultural experiment station in Geneva continued to discourage anyone who asked about *vinifera* and persisted in discounting Frank's claims of success. The official published and often repeated view from Geneva and Cornell was that small successes could be explained by mild weather, fortunate location and plain good luck. If Dr. Frank was successful for a few seasons, it was an anomaly—growing *vinifera* on a commercial scale in New York was not possible, it was a huge financial risk and time would illustrate that. In spite of success through the record cold winters of the late '50s and early '60s, the experts were certain that the *vinifera* "experiment" would eventually fail. Konstantin continued to plant and establish his vineyards, to grow *vinifera* with extraordinary harvests and to develop more and better rootstock/ scion combinations. In spite of these record harvests and continuing success, officials at Geneva discounted his claims, suggesting to some that the results might be overstated. So, Konstantin found reputable people to

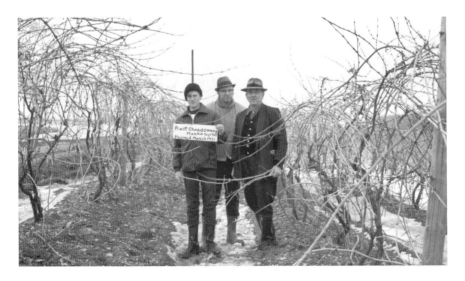

Fred Frank, Willy Frank and Dr. Frank in the vineyard, 1971.

observe harvests and swear on signed statements witnessed by a notary to the number, size and weight of clusters collected from a single vine.[77] Then he would produce these notarized testaments to anyone who questioned his results or his figures.

Charles Fournier once estimated that over the years, Konstantin, Eugenia and Walter Volz, along with helpers from the Gold Seal days, made more than 250,000 grafts.[78] The results would be measured in field trials in which the number and size of grape clusters, quality of the grapes and winter hardiness all were evaluated. Dr. Frank compared the volume and quality of the wine produced by individual graft combinations that showed promise, measuring the weight of grape clusters; recording the sugar and acid content; and making, testing and tasting literally hundreds of small batches of wine and then relating those outcomes to specific grafts grown in specific soils.[79] As he produced better combinations of grafts, he made these available to others through his nursery. He also provided what can be best described as a policy of open-ended internships. Interested people would come to Vinifera Wine Cellars and learn from Konstantin, and he freely shared what he knew.

Changing Tastes and Fine Wine

Even as the promise of Konstantin's work began to be taken seriously, American tastes for wine were going through something of an awakening. In 1950, the population of the United States was 152,271,417, and in that year, 140 million gallons of wine were sold in the United States (about 0.92 gallons of wine per person). Only about 36 million gallons (about 25 percent) of all wine sold was table wine. The overwhelming majority of wine sold at the time was fortified sweet wine, what is commonly called "plonk" by knowledgeable wine drinkers. Over the next sixty years, the wine market changed dramatically. By 2010, 784 million gallons of wine were sold in the United States, and the population had grown to 308,745,538 (about 2.50 gallons per person), or a 170 percent increase in consumption. More remarkable is the change in the character of the wine. In 2010, some 678 million gallons of wine (more than 86 percent) sold in the United States was table wine.[80]

In retrospect, there are a number of factors that can be seen as contributing to the change. After Prohibition, there was a rekindled interest in winemaking. Many people had been making wine during Prohibition (each household was permitted to make two hundred gallons of wine for personal use) and had been buying *vinifera* juice from California. Also, many GIs returning from the European theater of war had tasted the wines of Italy, France, Germany and other countries and regions. Many more Americans traveled to Europe after the war and had their own experiences with European wines. Many of the returning soldiers and tourists found the typical American wines lacking when they came home, and so they turned toward imported wines. In 1961, Julia Child's book *Mastering the Art of French Cooking* was published and enjoyed unprecedented success for a cookbook. Innovations from people like Child and, later, Alice Waters introduced new approaches to fine food—some that routinely paired good food with fine wine. Julia used to enjoy a sip or two even as she prepared the food on television. Robert Mondavi's experience when traveling in France in 1962 convinced him that he could make wine as good as or better than what he tasted in France back home in California. The experiences of travel and immigration to America brought new food and new tastes to this country, and preferences also began to change.

In 1965, Robert Mondavi left his family's business and undertook a new venture. During the period before he opened his business, Mondavi set out to talk with people in the wine business in the United States and Europe. Among those he met with was Konstantin Frank. In his vision, Mondavi came to associate wine with sophistication, good food and the good life—but not a life beyond the reach of a typical American. His vision was as much about the life one *wanted* to lead as it was the wine, and so he set out to intentionally personify his vision—to live the good life. This view, supplemented by the work of other small vintners in California, gained traction, and the market for American table wine began to grow. Mondavi's efforts to define the good life led to an increased interest in the "wine life" as well, and this attracted many people to the business of growing grapes and making wine. Many of these people had money to spend and resources acquired in other businesses and so could buy or build wineries in anticipation of the growing market; however, it was also done out of a desire to be part of the winemaker's lifestyle. This interest was not limited to the West Coast, however, and in the East, Dr. Frank's efforts were being noticed as well.

As the market for wine grew, large companies began to purchase wineries that were producing fine wine to cash in on this new popularity, as well as to acquire the cachet of quality without the effort or expense of actually doing what it required. More vineyards of *labrusca* and French hybrids were planted, as these large, mostly publicly traded companies geared up for the growing trend in wine consumption. That they misread the trend would become evident in just a few years. By the end of the decade, the American taste for wine had started to shift from sweet to dry and from native grapes to varietals. The large companies had invested in wines with the greatest predictable markets and margins. They invested in the development of these markets even though the growth in their industry was in varietal table wines and not the more common sweet wines that they were then producing.

When the Twenty-first Amendment effectively ended Prohibition, it left regulating alcoholic beverages largely to the states (although it did retain certain regulatory oversight powers). The federal government did retain some licensing control, which evolved into a knot of regulations and permits that serves largely to frustrate new business and complicate existing businesses. After Prohibition, each state approached the regulation and distribution of alcoholic beverages in its own way, but it is fair to say that general distribution to consumers was and remains fairly tightly controlled through licensing and highly regulated distribution systems. Not to be outdone by Washington, D.C., many of the states constructed their own respective knots of regulations and permits. Currently, there are nineteen states still in the wholesale and retail liquor sales business in one fashion or another, from state-run liquor distribution systems to state-run retail liquor stores. In spite of the significant regulatory roadblocks before them, small wineries did appear across the United States, and over a period of time, some states began to recognize wine produced by small wineries as "agricultural products" and changed laws to allow them to sell their products directly to customers.

In 1968, Pennsylvania passed the Limited Winery Act, which allowed for commercial wineries to sell their products directly to wholesale and retail consumers. Wineries had operated in the commonwealth since the end of Prohibition but had to sell their products through the state-run monopoly of the Liquor Control Board (LCB). The new law provided small wineries the opportunity to sell their products outside the restrictive control of the LCB. Pennsylvania's bold shift toward the business of small wineries is important in that it influenced many other states to follow suit. Pennsylvania, at the time, was the fifth-largest producer of grapes in the United States. By 2005, there were at least 104 small wineries operating in the commonwealth of Pennsylvania.[81]

Around Pennsylvania, interested growers began to look for resources and advice as they looked to start up their winery operations. Many would look to Philip Wagner of Maryland for advice, and some would travel to Keuka Lake to meet Dr. Frank. Some learned from both men. Over the next few years, Dr. Frank would meet with, work with and travel to the farms of a number of people interested in starting their own wineries. He consulted with Edward Vandyke of Troy, professors from State College, Ralph Kulzer of Pittsburgh and Douglas Moorhead of North East, Pennsylvania, to name a few.

When Moorhead's son, Douglas, completed his active duty in the service and returned from Europe, he brought with him the desire to grow European varieties that produced the wine he had enjoyed while overseas. Douglas Moorhead Jr. came to the Vinifera Wine Cellars to work with Dr. Frank in the vineyards and during the harvest. He was convinced that *vinifera* would grow and thrive in Pennsylvania, where Lake Erie would temper the cold winter. In September 1969, Moorhead and his partner, Bill Konneth, opened Presque Isle Wine Cellars on the same day as did their neighbor, Penn Shore Vineyards; these became the first two wineries to open under the new law. Presque Isle Wine Cellars was engaged in growing *vinifera* alongside French hybrid varieties from the beginning. Konstantin also welcomed delegations from Pennsylvania State University to Vinifera Wine Cellars to show them his acres of *vinifera* and share the methods that allowed for his success. He was always the teacher and welcomed the opportunity to spread the word to interested parties.

Philip Wagner was also an important source of information for the growing interest in wine. Wagner's vision was not unlike Konstantin's—to make very good wine for regular people to enjoy with meals and to

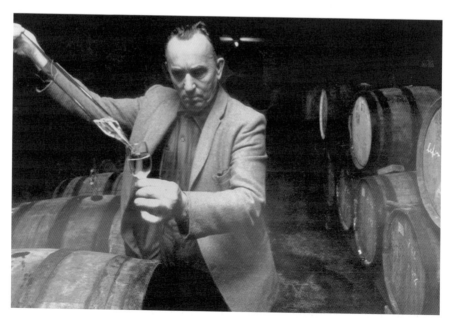

Dr. Frank with a wine thief in the barrel room at Vinifera Wine Cellars.

create the conditions where good wine is appreciated and enjoyed. In Maryland, Wagner's Boordy Wines had done well over the years, and Wagner had a leading voice in the small winery marketplace. His nursery sold French hybrid vines to commercial growers as well as home winemakers. In fact, many notable people from the emerging American fine wine movement, like Robert Mondavi and Warren Winarski, became friends of the Wagners. Charles Fournier, in particular, was a good friend of the Wagners and did a fair amount of business purchasing French hybrids from their nursery over the years. Like Konstantin, the Wagners sought out others with whom to share their expertise and to increase the number of growers of French hybrids. Many responded enthusiastically, and Philip Wagner's book remained in circulation for many years; used copies are still readily available today. Even Dr. Frank owned a copy of *American Wines and How to Make Them*, complete with handwritten margin notes. Unfortunately, Konstantin found no room for French hybrids in his vision of what could be excellent wine. He believed not only that French hybrids were just inferior grapes for wine but also that they would not survive the assault of phylloxera and were, in fact, toxic. He wrote letters to government officials, academicians, scientists and newspaper and trade editors detailing what he believed to be the toxic effects of French hybrid grapes and the presence of diglucosides, a chemical associated with pigmentation in plants. In his many talks and presentations, he included his concerns and criticisms of the toxic character of these wines.

Diglucoside Debacle

In general, *Vitis labrusca*, *Vitis riparia* and other native grapes contain diglucosides, whereas *Vitis vinifera* does not, containing only monoglucosides instead. In the process of hybridization, the associated diglucoside gene is dominant, so hybrid grapes will all have diglucosides as well as monoglucosides. The vigor and lower production costs of hybrids were thought to be a threat to the traditional and more expensive production of European varieties. Germany, France and other nations began testing imported vines and wine for diglucosides because it served as a reliable indicator of hybrid, non-*vinifera* grapes and wine.[82] Konstantin eventually came to believe, as some in Europe did at the time, that the presence of diglucosides presented a very real risk of breaking down into cyanide compounds in the fermentation or aging process and that the diglucosides could be directly linked to birth defects or other toxic effects.

At the time, there was an active and ultimately successful movement in parts of Europe to ban French hybrid grapes as substandard. As part of the effort, a number of arguments were raised, including health risks from diglucosides. Subsequent studies in the United States did not find the diglucosides to pose any measurable risk. Eventually, it was shown that the science behind these arguments was poor at best and nonexistent at worst. The reason for the European disapproval of French hybrids was to protect the quality of European wines from the perceived poorer quality and greater production of French hybrids. French hybrids often have a more vigorous growth and produce more juice than *vinifera*, but European winemakers and enthusiasts shared Konstantin's view that the resulting wines were substandard. Winemakers and growers in the traditional winemaking regions were concerned about cross-contamination between the pollen of the *Vitis vinifera* and the hybrids, and this led to them being banned in many places. Still, Konstantin railed against the French hybrid grapes as being toxic and unhealthy, although the science behind the argument had been discredited.

In response to one of the many letters he wrote, an official from the Department of Health Education and Welfare reported that they had indeed checked with many of the countries Dr. Frank said had prohibited growing hybrid grapes and found that they "have done so to protect their industries and not because of any toxicity of the grapes or the wine. We note that even the countries whose scientists have done the experimental work on hybrid grapes have not prohibited these grapes because of toxicity, if they have prohibited them at all."[83] This made little difference to Konstantin, however, and he continued to deride what he saw as second-rate grapes and second-rate wine.

His vigorous pursuit of this issue once again brought him into direct conflict not only with the scientists at Cornell but also with the wine production industry itself. The large eastern wine companies all used some French-American hybrids. The nascent table wine movement that was already underway in the eastern United States when Konstantin landed in New York was based on French hybrid varieties that were championed by Philip Wagner, founder and owner of Boordy Wines in Maryland. Philip Wagner had championed the French-American hybrid and built the reputation of Boordy Wines using them, as had others. He took Dr. Frank's words as a direct challenge and rose to defend his life's work and his product. If Dr. Frank was saying that the products of these companies and small wineries were all to be considered toxic on the basis of fairly suspect science, Wagner was not going to let the charge go unanswered.

Wagner began his own campaign of articles, letters and talks to defend the French hybrid and to discredit Konstantin's claims. Wagner saw Dr. Frank's characterization of French hybrid grapes and wines made from them as being threats to human health as direct and unsubstantiated threats to his business and his life's work, as well as just plain wrong. He worked to refute Dr. Frank's arguments at every turn, writing to scientists who were looking at the issue and encouraging them to publicly report their findings to combat the arguments from Europe and in the United States. Dr. Frank, however, was equally adamant and never shy about advancing his own argument, and the two traded competing arguments for years to come. These exchanges often put Charles Fournier, a friend to both of them, squarely in the middle.

Both Wagner and Frank frequently complained to their mutual friend about the other. In his letters to Wagner, Fournier tries to act as a good friend to both men and seeks a middle ground. In one letter, he wrote to Wagner that his friend Kotja (his name for Frank) was angry over remarks Wagner was reported to have made about the poor condition of the *vinifera* vines nearest the road at his winery. Fournier cautioned that Wagner should know that these were experimental vines and had not performed well, an outcome to be expected occasionally when conducting research. These were not the robust *vinifera* vines from which Frank's excellent wine was made. In another letter, Wagner complained to Fournier, noting that he (Fournier) had the influence necessary and should stop Frank from telling everyone that hybrids were toxic. Dr. Frank would complain publicly that the French hybrid wines were not good enough for Americans, and Wagner would argue that Dr. Frank's facts were wrong. Wagner would write to Fournier to complain of some new outrage committed by Dr. Frank, and Dr. Frank would express his feelings about Wagner's criticisms of his vineyards or his argument.

It was a very public disagreement, with ardent supporters of Wagner and Frank lining up to defend or disparage as the circumstances required. The truth, however, was likely far less stark. In fact, most winemakers were generally interested in what worked best on their farm, in their process and for their customers rather than in the "all or nothing" approach demanded by Dr. Frank. Wagner and Frank continued to disagree in person, in letters and in print until Konstantin's death in 1985. Later, Wagner always remembered their relationship as contentious but friendly. Fournier maintained as neutral a position as he could and remained friends with both men until his own death. He must have been frustrated given that these two important men could have been allies if not friends. Philip Wagner and Dr. Frank shared many goals. Wagner once wrote to Fournier, "I think it is time we begin to treat American

Wine as an object of honest discussion as we treat music, literature and the theatre. American wine-making will not have come of age until it can expect and welcome such discussion."[84] It is likely that Konstantin would have fully agreed so long as he did not know it was Wagner who wrote it.

In the end, it may be that Dr. Frank parsed the issues of French hybrids more finely than others could appreciate. In a letter to Harry Showalter written in 1971, he wrote that "I never says [sic] that the French hybrids are toxic. I say that twenty European scientists published their proofs that these hybrids are toxic. These French hybrids are prohibited the world over. They are prohibited not because they are hybrids, but because they are special kind of hybrids." He explained that "there are three kinds of hybrids. European hybrids where both parent plants are European verities—*Vitis vinifera*. The American Hybrids, but because they are special kind of hybrid's where one of the parents must be *Vitis labrusca* and the other can be European variety *Vitis vinifera*. Here in this case nobody say this hybrid could or should be toxic. And we have a third kind of hybrid which we call French hybrid." He noted that the term "French hybrid" had nothing to do with where the hybrid was from but rather was so named because "the parent plants used for breeding are other American species except *Vitis labrusca*."[85]

He also wrote of his concern with French hybrids facilitating the life cycle of the phylloxera louse: "It is well known that the leaves of Vinifera varieties, as well as the leaves of the American-Labrusca varieties cannot be attacked by the destructive race of root louse, so called 'leaf form Phylloxera'....The leaves of the Franco-American, so-called French Hybrids will be very badly attacked by the 'leaf form Phylloxera.' Therefore only in the planting of the French hybrids can the phylloxera make a full development cycle."[86] He makes an argument that to include French hybrids is to invite the phylloxera pest into the vineyard. He noted that even the native rootstocks on which the *vinifera* are grafted are only resistant to the phylloxera pest, not immune, and that such resistance varies.

So, perhaps, for Konstantin, French hybrids were a special subset of hybrids. He went on to extol the virtues of European and American hybrids but noted that hybrids with *labrusca*, while not toxic, still tend to suffer from the "foxy" *labrusca* taste. However, these finer points were rarely, if ever, made in his more public criticisms of toxic wines from French hybrids. Ironically, the question remains that as a scientist, he must have appreciated that the research did not agree with or support his proclamations. His refusal to accept the science and discontinue the diglucoside harangue is difficult to square with a man who devoted so much to the science of viticulture. If he did realize his mistake, it made little difference; he continued to criticize winemakers who would use what he saw as substandard grapes to make what could only be substandard wine when the *vinifera* alternative was available. This obstinate refusal to accept facts served to alienate many people in the business and isolated Konstantin from all but those most enthusiastic or forgiving admirers.

Frank was also writing and speaking to anyone who would listen about cheap, adulterated "European" wine. He wrote still more letters to state and federal authorities protesting the use of Baycovin or dimethyl dicarbonate (DMDC) in wine and, of course, the deleterious effects of French hybrids. This chemical was authorized for use in wine in the early 1970s in the United States and Germany. It was a very effective chemical for sterilizing wine during bottling. It was soon discovered that there were several undesirable reaction products that resulted from its use. In addition to unwanted changes in the aroma, highly reactive products formed that when combined with substances routinely found in wine would create toxic and carcinogenic compounds. At the same time, European firms were dumping cheap and often substandard wine on the U.S. market. Much of this wine was watered down or adulterated to make it palatable to the relatively unsophisticated tastes of new American wine enthusiasts. Konstantin complained about the cheap, poor-quality wine being sold under labels of fictitious chateaus or with pseudo-Renaissance paintings of saints. He frequently wondered why the federal government would allow such obvious substandard products into the country.

In addition, even after Baycovin was banned in the United States, it was still being used in the Algerian wine that was imported and sold in the United States. He wrote many letters to officials in Albany and in Washington apprising them of the continued presence of the banned chemical in the imported wine. Dr. Frank's early concerns and warnings proved to be correct, although the official position was that the quantities of these compounds were believed to be quite small. Government and industry officials declared that the levels of toxins in the wine were well within the safety thresholds of the time, but prudence alone, rather than substantive risk, required that the practice be stopped. Eventually, newer chemicals were created that served the purpose without the toxic side effects.

American Wine Society

Ultimately, the simple wine tastings and presentations did not generate the change that Konstantin wanted. On October 7, 1967, more than two hundred wine enthusiasts gathered at Dr. Frank's home for the purpose of organizing the American Wine Society (AWS). Dr. Frank explained to those assembled at his home the mission of the society: "This organization, composed of those individuals who enjoy wine and who are sincerely interested in the promotion and growth of superior quality domestic wines, would not be a commercial venture in any way. Our objective would be to inform the general public of the ability and natural resources to produce excellent wines here in our own country. Too frequently they are led to believe that the only fine wines are imported wines." On December 3, 1967, a smaller group met again at Frank's home, and the American Wine Society was officially constituted, with A.W. Laubengayer as president and Dr. Konstantin Frank as founder and technical advisor. The society was formed to promote wine to interested consumers through education and to advance wine quality and appreciation through competition among both professional and amateur winemakers. Today, the AWS boasts members in forty-one states and more than 120 chapters. Membership is open to consumers, professional and amateur winemakers and educators—the common denominator being the appreciation of wine—and it is the oldest organization of its type in the United States.

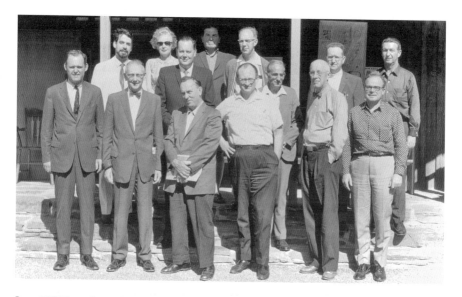

June 1968 board meeting of the American Wine Society. *Front row, left to right*: Walter Taylor, Aldus Fogelsenger, Dr. Konstantin Frank, Herman Laubengayer and Ken Proctor; the last man's name is unknown. *Back row, from left to right*: Mr. Axtel, Mrs. Danenhauer, Mr. Borgstedt, Mr. Danenhauer, Harold Applegate, Hamilton Mowbray, H.A. Kerr and Tom Clark. Elmer Philips is not present.

Konstantin was by now well known as a champion for *vinifera*. He enjoyed the attention and accolades of success that came his way. He brooked no middle ground, and as a result, he is remembered by some as difficult, obstinate and argumentative and often as a self-promoting egotist. To one degree or another, he was all of these things. Perhaps those attributes were necessary in combination with his technical expertise to bring his vision to the notice of the public. The willingness to buck the system and put one's reputation and personal wealth on the line is likely only found in someone of such temperament. Some of his critics claim that he was also a charlatan, but this he definitely was not. He understood from his days under the Soviet system how bureaucracies can crush innovation and silence the innovator. He saw firsthand at Gold Seal the impact of publicity and influence, and so he believed that to be heard, one must be noticed. He also knew that he was not a young man and that this was his moment to be heard—he was determined to make the best of it. His efforts were meant to teach Americans and lead them to what he understood to be better choices, better wines and, ultimately, a better life. He believed that this was a gift he could give to his adopted country.

By this time, Konstantin had embraced his new country completely. From the day he moved into his home on the hill above Keuka Lake, an American flag proudly flew every day. Once, when a visitor was about to take a picture of the house and winery from the vineyard, Konstantin noticed that the flag was not up and stopped the photograph from being taken until he could go back to the house and raise it. When he purchased barrels for his wine operation, he

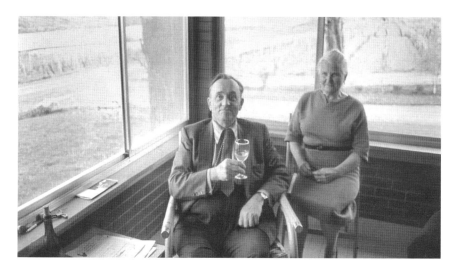

Dr. Frank and Eugenia in their home by Keuka Lake.

insisted, counter to winemaking practice, that the barrels be made of American oak and not the more traditional and accepted French oak.

He understood that there was no wine culture to rely on such as the one he had grown up in or the one that was common in Europe. To provide what was lacking, he drew on other interested people to search for a way to educate the American public in matters of wine. Somehow a cadre of wine lovers and oenophiles found its way to his door. Many of them were astonished to find not just thriving *vinifera* but also wines of an excellence on par with what they had come to believe was only produced in Europe. Dr. Frank's wines sold for a bit more than most other American wines, but he explained that they were true varietals—estate bottled and not sweetened or blends of juices from different grapes. The quality was worth the small premium of a somewhat higher price.

The enthusiasts heard the word, tasted the wine and spread the word. Many wine lovers and other winemakers took vacations to come and volunteer to work with Dr. Frank to learn more about wine and winemaking. Some went on to operate their own wineries; others became champions and defenders of their teacher. In an article in the *Chicago Tribune* in February 1969, J.H. Black of the State University of New York College at Geneseo is quoted as saying:

> *Dr. Frank is not impartial. He cannot be blamed for his anxiety to demonstrate while he gives away the priceless gift to an as yet unappreciative industry. Costs for Dr. Frank are almost tantamount to a bloodletting. He has invested his total capital and his whole heart into Vinifera Cellars and its mission…my wish is for understanding of Dr. Frank…to examine his teaching with care to improve the wine quality of a continent. I hope that it may occur before all we have of Dr. Frank is his writing and his wine.*[87]

It is unlikely that anyone could have foreseen the scale of the shift in the wine market that was already underway in the United States at this time. Whether Dr. Frank recognized this opportunity or not, he was committed to the idea that Americans deserved to have the very best of everything, including wine. Dr. Frank was as patriotic an American as one could find. Perhaps it was his time under the Soviet system, his experience as a refugee, the discovery of the possibilities of his adopted homeland or a combination of all of these, but Konstantin Frank loved the United States. This nation was the land of plenty, and he often said, "This country should have the very best. Where else do you find one house, four people, and four cars?" He could not understand why Americans, who could have the very best, would regularly settle for what he knew to be inferior wines since, in his mind, Americans deserved "only excellence."

The "Genevans"

As he grew older, his letters to politicians and agency bureaucrats grew more pointed, encouraging them to see what he could see and to work for the changes necessary to provide Americans with quality wine. In his letters, he made no efforts to be political or collegial and bluntly stated what he believed to be so, regardless of the cost to others. In various letters, he noted that scientists at the Geneva Experiment Station had been wasting money on studies that promote inferior French hybrid varieties and that major importers and distributors were playing on American ignorance of wine and selling inferior wine at premium prices. His letters were personal in both tone and content. For example, he wrote to Governor Hugh Carey of New York and complained that specific scientists from the Geneva station were wasting money traveling to Chile and Argentina to study growing *vinifera* when they were doing everything they could to prevent it from being grown here at home. He noted that scientists from the Geneva station could not learn anything about growing grapes in New York on a trip to Chile because the climate, soils and conditions were not at all comparable. In his letters, he named the scientists he found at fault and declared that if they wanted to know about *vinifera*, they only had to drive down the lake and he would tell them.[88]

By the mid-1960s, the difference of opinion that started when he first arrived at the Geneva station had grown to a full-scale public fight. The powers that managed the Geneva station, with its respected bulletins and advice to farmers, continued to publicly ignore Dr. Frank's work and maintained the recommendations for growing native and French hybrid grapes only. Dr. Frank pushed back as vigorously as he could and took every opportunity to demonstrate that those in Geneva were wrong or were "brainwashed." He held up each success, each award and every accolade for the world to see to underscore that the advice from Geneva was wrong. In turn, officials from Geneva quietly wrote letters and talked about the "vinifera experiment" as an interesting attempt that was doomed to eventual failure. They tended to ignore his successes but eagerly reported any sign of failure.

Friends and business acquaintances counseled Dr. Frank to tone down his attacks and to confine his public remarks to promoting his own wines and successes, without the vitriol and undermining of the products and work of others. Unfortunately, he continued to attack the quality of his competitors and raise issues of toxicity and the poorer quality of blended or sweetened wines. The list of his complaints and dissatisfactions seemed to grow and threatened to obscure his message that commercial production of the *vinifera* was more than just possible—it was a reality. However, for Dr. Frank, it was a zero-sum game—there were only winners and losers. He used his success and the recognition he gained as a way of denigrating his detractors, all the while pointing out their shortcomings and errors. Every success that he achieved was more proof that his critics were wrong and he was right. Each slight, real or otherwise, from the experiment station was more fuel to the fire. Competitors and others who found themselves targets of his criticism reacted as one might expect—they pushed back.

The "Genevans," as Dr. Frank referred to the staff of the experiment station, were slow to acknowledge his successes. Managers and winemakers at the other wineries gave him the cold shoulder and waited for the anticipated satisfaction of that one really cold winter that they were sure would come to the Finger Lakes. But the *vinifera*, following the methods Dr. Frank used, survived and, in some cases, did much better than native and French hybrid grapes. The 1960s were spent solidifying the early successes and expanding the *vinifera* plantings. Colder than normal winters reoccurred several times in the 1960s, and there were losses of *vinifera*, but in general, these losses were consistent with the experience in the winter of 1956–57. Losses of more than 20 percent occurred in both Gold Seal's and Dr. Frank's vineyards, but similar or even greater losses were found among the French hybrids. Interestingly enough, losses in the 40 percent range were found in some Concord vineyards. Both sides of the *vinifera* discussion claimed that their points had been made, and the disagreement continued unabated. In point of fact, though, Konstantin had proven that his methods and his ideas would work—*Vitis vinifera* could be grown on a commercial scale in the Finger Lakes in a cold climate.

Fred Taylor, who was president of the Taylor Wine Company during this time, wrote to Konstantin in 1964 with news that he had heard from Geneva of significant losses of *vinifera* during the winter of 1963–64. Dr. Frank wrote back a thoroughly researched and documented reply noting that the killing was from one of several fungal infections and that low winter temperatures could exacerbate the losses. He described at length how vines die from cold and how the losses to which Taylor referred were not actually cold related. He also noted that the death of vines from the fungi were not limited to his vineyards but indeed seen throughout the region and in all *labrusca* vines, as well as the *vinifera*. In fact, his work indicated that fungi were the underlying cause of as much as 50 percent of the losses ascribed to cold temperatures in the years from 1957 to 1963. "This mistaken diagnosis can be dangerous," Konstantin warned Taylor. "Such a mistake could mislead the grape growers, cause the destruction of their crop and advance these diseases."[89]

He detailed to Taylor the required treatment to control the fungal infections and, uncharacteristically, did not go on the offensive, blaming the people at the Geneva station. Instead, he argued for greater transparency between growers and scientists to encourage knowledge and scientifically based management strategies offered by the station. He went on to argue that the region has significant potential for growing table grapes as well as wine using the varieties developed by the scientists at the Geneva station.

Predictably, tensions between Konstantin and his wine-producing neighbors also grew strained. At the time, these neighbors included Taylor Wine and Gold Seal. His constant railing about French hybrids and friction with the Geneva station caused stress between him and his neighbors, and as one might imagine, it took something of a toll on him as well. In 1972, Dr. Frank wrote to Frederick Schroeder, the new Pleasant Valley Wine Company managing director, with something of an olive branch. "With the intent and purpose to eliminate any misunderstandings that may exist between ourselves, I would very much like to invite you to visit my vineyards and wine cellar." He asked Schroeder to extend the invitation to others at the company, including "my old friend Mr. Charles Fournier." He appealed to their common interests: "Inasmuch as we are all in the same venture, but on vastly different scales, it is my sincere feeling that discussion and understanding of our respective activity and general philosophy would be worthwhile and perhaps benefit the Finger Lakes Wine industry…I am sure there are a number of areas in which a discussion can go far in resolving some differences of the past."[90]

Mr. Schroeder responded favorably but declined to invite others, thinking instead that "a direct invitation from you would be more proper."[91] This is an uncommon glimpse into Konstantin's desire for better relations with others in the industry. He was apparently using the occasion of Mr. Schroeder's recent promotion to managing director of the Pleasant Valley Wine Company to mend some badly worn fences, but little progress was made. Since his days at Gold Seal, Dr. Frank had pursued his vision with little regard for the feelings or interests of others. For many, Dr. Frank was and would remain "the madman on the hill." All but his most ardent supporters winced at his treatment of those who had criticized him or had simply elected to go along with the accepted wisdom of their day. Now, at seventy-three years old, he reached out to colleagues, but many of those had been subject to what they considered ridicule and disaffection. For the most part, there was little interest in reaching back and patching up old wounds.

Meanwhile, he continued to experiment and grow *vinifera* on the hillsides above Keuka Lake, and his efforts were drawing still more attention. In

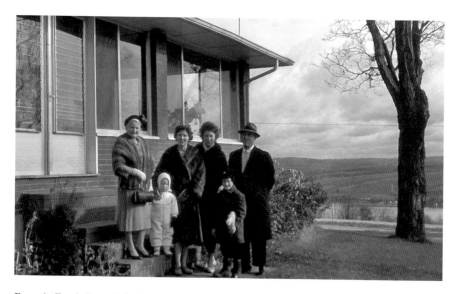

Eugenia Frank, Lena Schelling, Hilda Volz and Dr. Frank with young Heide Schelling and Donald Schelling.

a memo of January 11, 1973, John P. Tomkins, of the Department of Pomology at Cornell University, wrote to colleagues at the New York State College of Agriculture (NYSCA) at Cornell that despite having "rather fixed opinions as to his motives, problems, frustrations and successes, I really believe that many of us working with grapes had better give some thought to the fact that Dr. Konstantin Frank might be 25 to 50 years ahead of us in his thinking about grapes for New York State."[92] Tomkins appears to have been an early believer in Dr. Frank among the staff at the Geneva Experiment Station and at Cornell. Bulletins and reports being produced by the Geneva station began to include cautious remarks and observations about *vinifera*. It was even acknowledged, though grudgingly, that there might be a place for *vinifera* in the Finger Lakes grape region. In the 1960 report *Cultural Practices for Commercial Vineyards*, the subject of *vinifera* is given only four sentences. In the reissue of the report in 1973, only two paragraphs (eight sentences) out of seventy-two pages of content are given over to *vinifera*. For the most part, the same warnings about risk and failure are repeated, and after more than twenty years of results, none of the results of the Gold Seal and Dr. Frank experience is mentioned. Change, when it comes, often comes slowly.

Part IV

COMING OF AGE

THE WINE REVOLUTION

The shift in American preferences for better-quality wines was well underway by the mid-1970s. While per capita wine consumption was increasing, the mix of wine products was moving to drier, more food-friendly wines and away from the sweet, highly alcoholic wines that had characterized American wine production since Prohibition. These trends of changing food preferences and increased awareness of wine—which, for the most part at that time, meant imported and most likely French wine—had created a new demand for fine wine. Savvy distributors understood the trend and quickly began to market inexpensive wines with pretentious or attractive labels to the largely inexperienced American wine buyer. Many Americans were buying table wines for the first time and had little or no experience with which to judge or choose what they would buy. Marketers capitalized on the lack of knowledge by packaging wines especially for this new market using labels with Renaissance-like pictures of saints and with names that seemed to be French or at least vaguely European.

Dr. Frank decried any wine he deemed substandard, whether French hybrid, native grape or lesser European/Algerian wine. Many imported wines were being sold to Americans as European but were actually from Algeria. Frank complained that if you put a saint or a nun on the label and gave it a vaguely European-sounding name, Americans would buy it. These products were simply not good enough for Americans. "The greatest nation on Earth deserves the greatest wine," he would say, and it was his mission to bring it to them.[93] He found the cheap European wines being imported through Algeria particularly offensive and wrote to government and business officials to share his feelings.

With the growing interest came an inevitable learning curve. The tastes and the preferences of consumers new to the world of wine progressed slowly, since the traditions of wine were all but nonexistent and the resources to learn about wine were few and far between. This was to change quickly in the coming decades, and Konstantin was situated to become an important part of this new interest. So it was one evening early in 1971 that Konstantin answered a knock on the back door of his home to find a young man with long hair and a beard standing there. "What do you want?" Konstantin asked suspiciously. "I want to learn about wine," the visitor replied. After a slight hesitation, Konstantin said, "Well, if you want to learn about wine, you might as well start at the beginning." He directed the visitor to the cold garage, where he was in the process of grafting vines. He showed his visitor how to make the precise cuts, match up the scion and root just so and coat the graft with wax to protect the wound. As they sat there, Konstantin had his young pupil read from various newspaper and magazine clipping written about him and the superiority of *vinifera* grapes. In the feeble warmth of a small electric heater, Konstantin directed the grafting and interrupted the young reader to underscore particularly important parts of the articles. Kevin Zraly was nineteen years old in 1971 when he came to the Finger Lakes to learn about wine.

Zraly was attending college in downstate New York and working part time as a bartender at a restaurant with a growing reputation for fine food. Eventually, he was asked to take over managing the beverage operation, including the buying of wine. He realized that he did not know enough about wine, and so he set out to learn. One night, he met Walter Taylor, owner of Bully Hill Vineyards, and after some conversation, Taylor invited him to come to Bully Hill and learn about New York State wines. Walter Taylor was committed to making quality wines, but he approached the challenge using hybrids, not *vinifera*. Taylor allowed Zraly to stay in a guest cottage on the vineyard and introduced him to winemaking in the Finger Lakes. Taylor also suggested that before his visit was over, he should go down the hill and meet Dr. Frank. "But," he warned with a smile, "don't tell him you are staying up here or he may throw you out."

After his first visit and lessons on grafting, Zraly came back the next day and the next and then began to come back as often as his college classes and work schedule would allow. He helped with the grafting all winter, and he helped to plant the vines on his hands and knees through the spring. He worked in the vineyards and in the cellars doing whatever Konstantin directed him to do and learning all the time. Over the next year or so, Zraly would work under the exacting direction of Dr. Frank in every phase of producing wine.[94]

Eugenia did not like Kevin's long hair and beard and at first discouraged Konstantin from working with him and inviting him into their house. Konstantin continued to work with his protégé but would, from time to time, ask him to get a haircut and shave. Eugenia did not like the idea of a hippie being seen at the house, but Konstantin enjoyed working with him. Still,

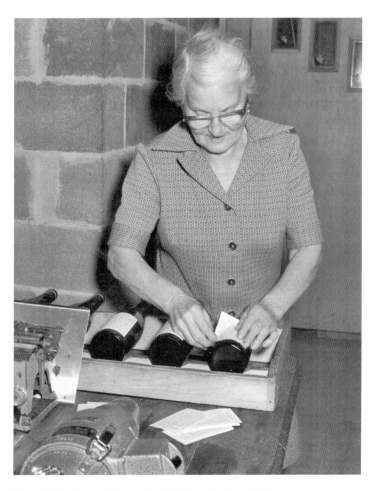

Eugenia Frank carefully putting labels on bottles of wine.

Eugenia did not like young Kevin coming onto the breezeway or into the house for a glass of wine after a day at work in the vineyard or on the bottling line. So, occasionally, Konstantin and Kevin would share a bottle of wine behind the garage out of sight from Eugenia, tipping back the bottle for a swallow and passing the bottle back and forth.

Zraly wanted to include Dr. Frank's wine on his restaurant wine list, but without a distributor, purchases had to be made directly from the winery. He would pick up a few cases on his frequent visits, but his small car limited the amount he could carry. Zraly would have to arrange for a trucking company to pick up the small load and deliver it downstate to the restaurant. Deliveries were difficult to schedule and unreliable. Eventually, he bought a van so he could buy the wine and deliver it to the restaurant himself. Customers of the restaurant began to ask where they could buy this wine made in New York, and some, following Zraly's direction, would drive to the winery for a taste. After graduation from college, Zraly continued his self-education in all things wine by traveling to California and then to Europe and other international wine regions to meet winemakers, visit wine regions and learn about wine.

When he was only twenty-five years old, Kevin Zraly was hired as the wine manager of the Windows on the World restaurant on the top of the World

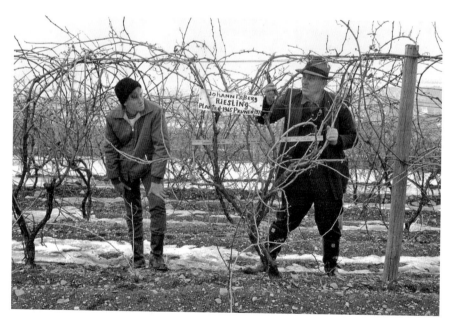

Fred Frank and Dr. Frank in winter vineyards, 1971.

Trade Center. He oversaw the business of a wine list that included more than eight hundred wines from around the world. From there, he started the Windows on the World wine course, which led to the book of the same name. The *Windows on the World Complete Wine Course* is the most popular book on wine ever written. After the tragedy of September 11, 2001, at the request of the Windows on the World extended family and friends, Zraly relocated the school and continued to teach the wine course under its original name. Even today, when he teaches the course, he uses a Dr. Frank's Vinifera Wine Cellar Riesling in one of the lessons.

Zraly's stop at Dr. Frank's door could not have been timed better. American tastes were turning toward better wine, and as more people began to buy table wine, some saw opportunities to become winemakers. Both the consumers and newly minted winemakers were on steep learning curves. Efforts to grow *vinifera* had historically failed in the eastern United States, but that did not stop new attempts from being made. Dr. Frank's success and willingness to share his knowledge brought a steady stream of enthusiasts to his door. He worked with vineyard managers and winemakers from across the eastern United States, especially Virginia, and helped to found the Vinifera Growers Association in 1973 (now called the Atlantic Seaboard Wine Association).

Ascendancy of American Wine

As Americans began to enjoy better wine, they frequently turned to European wines, as most "quality" wine meant imported wine to many of them. Meanwhile, perfectly good wines produced in the United States, primarily in California, were struggling to compete. In 1976, the unthinkable happened. On May 24, a blind wine tasting was held featuring ten wines from the United States, all from California, and eight wines from France. The judges were selected from among the cognoscenti of French wine and had been invited to participate by Steven Spurrier, the owner of a Paris wine shop and school, and his primary instructor, Patricia Gallagher. The tasting was conducted in two stages—first the Chardonnays and then the Cabernet Sauvignons. In the first round, every French judge selected an American Chardonnay, though not necessarily the same American Chardonnay, as the best wine. The consternation only grew when an American Cabernet received the most overall points in the second round. No one expected such a result. Even though critics of how the tasting was conducted sprang up almost as quickly as the news went out, in general most of the judges eventually acknowledged that the scores reflected the quality of the wines they tasted that day. Suddenly, quality was no longer limited to European wine, and French wine no longer held the distinction of quality simply for being French.

In his book *Judgment of Paris*, George Taber analyzed the differences between French and American wines. Taber compared tradition versus experimentation and old-world techniques versus new-world innovation and technology to explore the reasons for the differences. He also exposed the concern as to whether the comparison of fairly young American wines was fair to the French, which reasonably might have been expected to improve with age to be better. While these are interesting to the enthusiast, the effect of the tasting was to immediately elevate not just the wines in the competition but every California wine and, indeed, the very process of winemaking. Robert Mondavi had been selling the wine life and the good life as one and the same. The tasting demonstrated that he was also selling excellence. Americans could look to their own winemakers and feel confident of quality.

Within the United States, the effect was less generous. *California* wines had been victorious on that day in Paris, not wines from New York or Virginia. Furthermore, the winning wines disappeared from shelves almost immediately. Nonetheless, American wine drinkers embraced their new wine country, and Napa Valley became the center of the U.S. wine world; everyone began to race to duplicate what would become "California style" Chardonnays and Cabernets. For new consumers unfamiliar with wine, a wine's origin in California, more particularly Napa, became the signal of quality. The California style of Chardonnay grew out of the attempt in the 1960s and '70s to duplicate the tradition of French white burgundies produced by barrel fermentation and aging in new oak barrels, which gives the wine characteristics of vanilla, butter, spice and perhaps toast and cedar, as well as a more full-bodied texture. Unlike most varietals, Chardonnay is something of a blank slate, so it reflects the terroir, the winemakers' decisions and the winemaking process more than other varieties that have more personality. With a shift in the method of production or a change in the process, the wine will reflect the change. What became known as the "California style of Chardonnay" was unlike the wines that had competed in the Paris tasting.

In 1976, there were 376 million gallons of wine sold in the United States, 228 million gallons of which (60 percent) were table wine. By 1986, consumption had grown to 587 million gallons, of which 487 million (about 83 percent) were table wine. This represents about a 40 percent increase in the market as a whole in ten years, but the market for table wine more than doubled. The public interest in wine was growing very quickly, and as one might expect, the average consumer was inexperienced. The public accepted California wines as benchmarks of quality, and many of them deserved such recognition. But Americans' appreciation for fine wine was generally as young as the marketplace, and the nature of wine was not immediately appreciated. Year-to-year variations are a natural aspect of wine since the weather varies from one year to the next. As an agricultural product, and one that bears a remarkable association to where it is grown and the weather of the year in which it is grown, natural variations are to be expected.

In places where wine is part of the culture, this natural variability is understood, but for much of the new wine-buying public, it was not. Americans, for the most part, purchase wine to drink; most wine in the United States is said to be consumed within forty-eight hours of being purchased. The concept of buying wine to be saved for consumption some years down the road was not generally understood or observed. In the new American wine marketplace, wine was purchased to be consumed, and some consistency from bottle to bottle was as important as consistency from year to year. Consumers were used to national restaurant chains and food products that tasted the same wherever and whenever they were purchased. The nature of fine wine as a reflection of the variability of the growing conditions was not immediately appreciated by most consumers.

The wine revolution was clearly underway when, in 1977, the Coca-Cola Company purchased the Taylor Wine Company and, within a few years, relocated the production to California. This was one of many acquisitions and attempts by companies not familiar with wine taking over wine businesses. Coca-Cola was familiar with the power of brand and therefore purchased a name as entry into what it saw as a growing and profitable market. What the large companies generally misunderstood was the nature of the product and the growing consumer interest and knowledge of wine quality. For the most part, the large companies simply got it wrong. Part of what was driving the new wine market was wine quality, but part of it was also what Robert Mondavi was selling: the wine life (in essence, an idea). For many consumers, every bottle of wine was, in a small way, their own sample of the wine life. The brand that was being purchased was richer and deeper than what the big beverage companies were selling.

When Taylor operations were moved to California, the market for New York grapes fell dramatically. The sudden loss of demand in the New York grape market resulted in growers having nowhere to sell their grapes, and many left their fruit on the vines to rot. The growers were not licensed to produce wine on their own. Most wine sales were made in what has been called the three-tiered system: producers sell to distributors or wholesalers who, in turn, sell to retail outlets that, in turn, sell to consumers. Small farms were not usually licensed as wineries primarily because of the costs involved, and if they were to produce wine, they would not find distributors because their production volumes were too small. With the loss of grape sales to the large wineries sales, growers were facing losses so steep that many simply did not bother to harvest their grapes. They had observed the early successes that the Pennsylvania Limited Winery Act had given small growers to their south, and after several years of poor grape sales and declining prices, New York State growers began to push for legislation that would simplify the permit process and enable them to make and sell their wine directly to consumers. In 1976, the activism and advocacy of grape growers paid off, and although there were only nineteen wineries in the state, the New York state legislature passed the Farm Winery Act.

Predictably, the liquor and wine industry opposed the legislation and suggested that the breakdown of the traditional system would ultimately work against the interests of the small farmers and consumers. They warned that allowing wine sales by small farmers would result in a loss of wine quality and a loss of sales for New York wines in general. In this instance, though, the legislative stars aligned, and with the support of the restaurant industry, Farm Bureau, the farm community in general and many other enthusiastic supporters, the bill passed. The legislation became the model for other similar pieces of legislation around the United States. The law allows a farmer to make and sell wine directly to consumers and also to liquor stores and restaurants. The ability to make direct sales created the opportunity for a "boutique winery" to make and sell wine directly to the public at a much lower permit cost. Before the law, a winery like Dr. Frank's Vinifera Wine Cellars producing fewer than ten thousand cases of wine annually was required to have the same permits and meet the same regulatory requirements as a Taylor or Gold Seal producing hundreds of thousands of cases of wine. The new law allowed for a less expensive permit for the farm winery. Over subsequent years, the act would be amended to allow for food to be served at wineries, limited off-site sales, wine to be sold on Sundays and other expansions.

In 1985, it was modified to require that 100 percent of New York State juice was necessary to call a wine "New York Wine," although in years of low harvests, special permission to use out-of-state grapes has been given.

To be considered a "Farm Winery," the operation could not produce more than 150,000 gallons, or about 60,000 cases of wine, annually. By 2013, there were more than three hundred wineries operating in New York State, with more than one hundred of them operating in the Finger Lakes. Coupled with changing tastes and preferences, the Farm Winery Act fueled the growth of the modern wine marketplace that thrives today. New York State is the third-largest producer of grapes in the United States after California and Washington. The majority of grapes are still grown for the grape juice and jelly market. It is, however, the second-largest wine producing state in the nation (third if you limit it to wine produced with only New York State grapes), bottling 38 million gallons of wine (about 16 million cases) in 2005. With this change in the law, small producers could begin to take their products directly to the marketplace, and with Dr. Frank's innovations, their products could be made from *vinifera* grapes. As the market grew, most attention has been given to the wines produced from *vinifera* varieties. Even though native and hybrid varieties vastly outnumber the acres of *vinifera* grown in New York, most new vineyards are planted with *vinifera*. The Farm Winery Act contributed to many small winemakers being able to enter the marketplace and embrace the promise of *vinifera* as envisioned by Konstantin Frank.

Changing of the Guard

Vinifera Wine Cellars was in an excellent condition to capitalize on the growing interest in wine. Konstantin had predicted for years that if Americans understood wine, they would value the wines made from *vinifera*. As the market began to expand, it seemed that the years of "missionary work" would finally pay off. Dr. Frank insisted on doing most of the Vinifera Wine Cellars business himself, from sales and marketing to winemaking and business management. In addition to the travel, this required many hours of preparing permit applications and maintaining exhaustive records. Although he wrote many letters, the general business correspondence often suffered in favor of subjects that Konstantin found more interesting. He would drop the work of managing his business for almost anything he found more interesting at the moment, and so the administration of the business suffered.

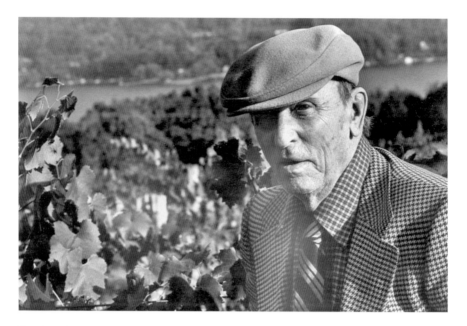

Dr. Frank in the Vinifera Wine Cellars vineyards.

Konstantin relied on Willy more and more to handle those aspects of the business he found tedious. Often he would call on Willy to assist when a deadline loomed or had passed, and Willy would step in to do what he could. Where Konstantin was a scientist, Willy was a businessman, so Konstantin continued to invite and encourage Willy to come to the Finger Lakes and join the business full time. Still, Willy remained reluctant to do so. Instead, he traveled the five hours or so from Long Island to the winery on many weekends to help his father in the vineyards, with the harvest or with bottling, but his attempts to become involved with management of the business were rebuffed. Although he had a degree in business, when his skills were used, it was only to put out fires caused by a missing report or missed deadline or to complete administrative tasks that his father ignored. He wrote letters, filed paperwork and supported his father in every way that he could and still maintain his independence. He was unwilling to join the business without a clearly defined role and hence likely suffer his father's difficult management style as Walter Volz had.

Konstantin reveled in his hard-earned success and the recognition that was showered on him. He would list the articles about him and kept a copy of every book in which he was mentioned, and on occasion, he might produce a book or two to demonstrate his claims to a visitor. He continued to pursue his vision as largely an experiment station, planting as many as sixty different varieties of *vinifera*. His technical work and his outreach activities often took precedence over routine business, such as recordkeeping and maintenance of the many permits and licenses required to operate a winery. In a 1966 letter to the company's lawyer, Willy wrote, "What a pity, Papa could have it so good if he would only give up trying to do everything his way and by himself. I did not think so before but now I am convinced that the best thing for Papa and the farm would be for him to semi-retire to his beloved research and wine making.... You know my position now, I and my Brother-in-law Walter are ready, it is up to Papa."[95] It would be nearly twenty years more before his father would reluctantly agree.

Dr. Frank's advisors encouraged him to do some planning for the disposition of the winery in the event of his death. He was, after all, in his seventies at this point, and some of the same traits and stubborn pride that led him to success were beginning to work against him. He may have believed that Willy would take over from him, and his successes would be forgotten. He was concerned that Willy's business skills would drive the decision-making at the winery toward profit alone without a deep concern for quality. While maintaining his life in New York City, Willy had become involved in the day-to-day business operations already at this time, keeping up with the regulatory requirements of permits and recordkeeping, writing letters to state officials to keep applications on track and responding to administrative issues that his father failed to do. Willy's efforts were often made in spite of his father. The business was not sustainable as it was being run by Konstantin, and father and son would frequently argue. Weekend visits frequently ended with flaring tempers and heated words. As he grew older, more details slipped from his grasp, but still Dr. Frank would not allow his son to come on board in a role that would include some degree of leadership or authority.

Eventually, at the urging of his lawyer, in 1972 Konstantin arranged for ownership to eventually pass equally to his three children: Willy, Hilda and Helene. Willy knew his father well enough to know that should he come on board, all of his actions and ideas would be subject first to his father and eventually to his sisters' approval. He told his father that he would not join the winery full time unless he had a controlling interest. Konstantin held up three fingers and said, "I have three children. Which one do I cut off?"[96] There would be no controlling interest. As the years passed and Dr. Frank's health began to falter, Willy reconsidered his decision but not his position. Willy and Margrit purchased some land on Seneca Lake near Watkins Glen

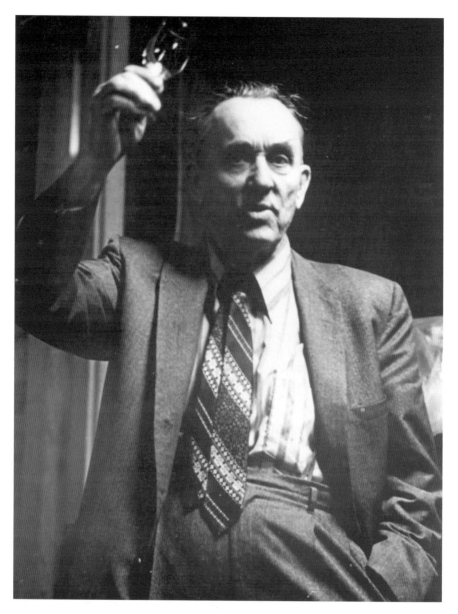

A toast from Dr. Frank.

in 1978 to plant their own vineyard. Now, on weekends, the family (Willy, Margrit and their children, Fred and Barbara) would drive five hours from Long Island to work their own vineyard. The land had been in grapes before but had not been worked for some time. The first task at hand was to clear the land in preparation for the *vinifera* grapes that would follow: Pinot Noir, Chardonnay and Pinot Meunier. The makings of classic champagne. Willy wanted to make wine but did not want to compete with his father, which he knew would have likely resulted in a still deeper rift between them.[97]

Willy and the children also continued to help at the Vinifera Wine Cellars when help was needed, but Konstantin showed no sign of giving up control. Now, though, age and the effects of diabetes were beginning to take a toll on the old man. He no longer had the same vigor that had permitted him to

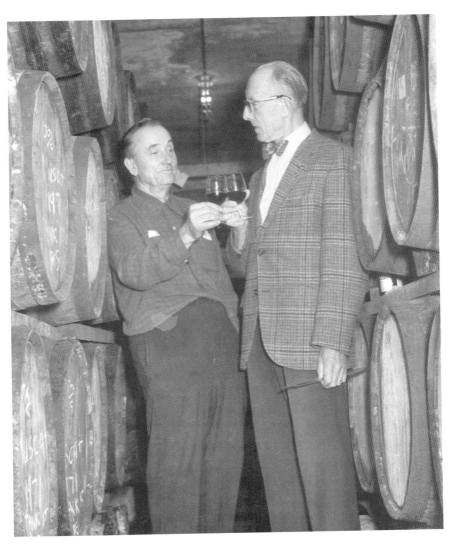

Dr. Frank and Charles Fournier in the barrel room at Vinifera Wine Cellars, 1972.

be winemaker, owner, vineyardist, chief scientist and the public face of the Vinifera Wine Cellars. Sales trips were less frequent, and his eyesight and palate began to fail him. While he had not been the best production and inventory manager in the past, those important functions began to receive still less attention now. The wine and the business suffered. Sales fell off, and cellar operations no longer received the attention they required. Walter Volz tried to take on more and more of the work that Dr. Frank had always done, but he did not have the winemaking knowledge or experience of his father-in-law or the desire to fight the old man at every turn.

Konstantin's flagging health became evident to his closest professional friends and allies at a meeting of the American Wine Society in Arlington, Virginia, in 1977. At this meeting, Philip Wagner, Lucie Morton and Robert de Treville Lawrence were on a panel to discuss "The Vine and Wine Experience in the East." Robert de Treville Lawrence, the first president of the Vinifera Growers Society, a solid supporter and cooperator of Dr. Frank's, aggressively criticized French hybrids as second rate and inferior, even going so far as to denigrate Philip Wagner personally. Wagner rose to give an eloquent argument for promoting all good wine, especially that made from French hybrids. He insisted that there was room for everyone in the Wine Society.

At the conclusion of their presentations and remarks, Dr. Frank stood in the audience and demanded a turn to contribute his own views on the subject. From the floor of the conference, he repeated his arguments that Americans deserved only the best and that necessarily meant wine from *vinifera* grapes. He gave a rambling and disparaging critique of their ideas (including the then discredited diglucoside complaint)[98] and went on to make his familiar claims of deleterious health effects of consuming juice and wine from French hybrids. His mind wandered from subject to subject before a few friends gently led him from the floor. His friends were embarrassed for him, and his detractors were angered anew. To those in attendance who knew him well, it was a signal that all was not well with their friend and mentor. The list of friends included Charles Fournier, Walter Taylor, Douglas Moorhead, Leonard Olson and Arnie Esterer, friends and "cooperators" of Frank's and all who were growers of French hybrids.[99] Wagner again wrote to Charles Fournier to complain about Frank and to caution him about associating with him. Fournier, of course, continued to support his friend Kotja while still growing French hybrids and making wine as part of the Gold Seal operations. It is believed that Fournier may have attempted to facilitate peace between his friends, but without much success.

"LEARN TO SHAVE ON ANOTHER MAN'S BEARD"

As Konstantin slowed down, the accolades continued to pour in. The Vinifera Wine Cellars' Chardonnay was singled out for a bicentennial luncheon in Boston honoring Queen Elizabeth II in July 1976. In 1979, he received a citation from Governor Hugh Carey of New York, who named March 7 of that year "Dr. Konstantin Frank Day" in honor of his success with *vinifera* but also because "[h]e cherishes the belief that only the best of the best is suitable for the palate of the American wine connoisseur, as well as the average consumer." That same year, Fred Frank (Willy's son and Konstantin's grandson) graduated from Cornell University with a degree in agricultural business. He had made a personal commitment to become part of the winery when he was much younger. Margrit Frank recalled her son saying to her on one of the many weekend trips to the winery, "I belong here," when he was about eleven years old. When it was time to go to college, there was no oenology or viticulture program on the East Coast, so Fred went to Cornell and majored in agricultural business. He took every wine-related course available at the time. When he graduated from Cornell in 1979, Konstantin encouraged him to come to the winery and begin to take over from him—this would have meant bypassing Willy for the top post.

His grandfather wanted Fred to come on board because he saw his grandson as a willing student and protégé, one who would not argue with him over every choice and decision as he expected Willy would. Willy, however, wanted his chance to run the winery, to bring his business skills to bear on the issues that he knew were threatening the viability of Dr. Frank's legacy. He discussed the situation with Fred and suggested that he go to work for another wine business to gain experience in the world, out from under the control of Dr. Frank and the insulating environment of the family business. "Learn to shave on another man's beard," he counseled his son.[100] Then, when he had gained experience and Willy had had an opportunity to manage the business, he could return to lead the family business. A plan of sorts emerged in which Fred would eventually manage the business of the Vinifera Wine Cellars; his sister, Barbara, would become the winemaker; and Eric Volz, Walter and Hilda's son, would manage the vineyards.

Not wanting to step in front of his father, Fred went from Cornell directly to work for Banfi Vintners, which was and remains an established producer and importer of Italian wines. At the time, it was the largest importer of wines into the United States. Fred was assigned to work in "crew drives," where salespeople were sent to generate business in underperforming areas of the country. For months, he lived out of his suitcase, working on sales and marketing projects in areas as diverse as Montana and the south side of Chicago. He learned sales on the streets and was rewarded for his results. Eventually, he was assigned as a state sales manager in New England. Working with six regional distributors and bolstered by Banfi's successful nationwide marketing and popular product line, Fred continued to do well.

After several years with Banfi, Fred began to look beyond his sales work with Banfi to learn more about the production side of wine. With his grandfather's help, he was accepted into the prestigious Geisenheim Institute in Germany as a visiting student. His undergraduate degree from Cornell University was sufficient to allow him to take only the upper-level classes in viticulture and oenology. All in all, Fred spent a year in Germany studying viticulture, wine and winemaking. On his weekends and breaks from school, he would travel around Europe, visiting the family wineries of fellow students from Geisenheim and visiting relatives. Friends encouraged him to buy a motorcycle because of the high cost of gas in Europe. So, Fred purchased a Yamaha RZ350, a type of racing motorcycle, for his weekend trips. Growing up, his father had not permitted Fred to have a motorcycle, and he was able to enjoy his new ride until a family friend showed his mother a photo of him on his Yamaha. The travels around Europe allowed him to see the vineyards, taste the wines and gain a perspective on the wine culture and traditions. The experience would underpin his commitment to the family business in years to come.

In 1983, after his year at Geisenheim, studying and traveling to the wine regions of Europe, Banfi contacted Fred with an offer. Banfi wanted to have a U.S. headquarters that reflected the values and stature of the Marianni family, proprietors of Banfi Wines. To that end, it had purchased a former Vanderbilt home situated on 127 acres in Old Brookville, New York. The owners of Banfi Wines asked Fred to come back and establish a vineyard on that property. Recognizing the opportunity to create a showcase vineyard for the once-in-a-lifetime assignment that it was, he eagerly accepted. In this role, he was able to bring all of his wine and business experience to bear. Fred continued to work on the Old Brookville Vineyard until his father asked him to join the family business in 1993.

Barbara Frank graduated from Cornell University in 1983 with a degree in pomology and a minor in food science. As an undergraduate student, she had completed an internship at Gold Seal in 1981 and received the New Jersey Shaulis Advancement of Viticulture Award in 1982 for viticultural research that she had conducted at the Geneva Experiment

Station. In 1983, she traveled to Germany and, like Fred, attended the Geisenheim Institute as a guest student in viticulture and oenology. Upon her return, she continued her studies at California State University–Fresno, graduating in 1988 with a graduate degree in oenology. During her time in California, Barbara completed an internship at Domaine Mumm, worked crushes at Schramsburg and Navarro and completed her thesis in conjunction with work completed with Domaine Chandon. After graduation, she began work as the assistant winemaker at S. Anderson Vineyards in Yountville, California.

As Barbara and Fred were learning the skills expected of them, Eric Volz was studying at the equally demanding school of Dr. Frank. Eric had attended the State University of New York–Morrisville and planned to transfer to the University of California to study viticulture, but his grandfather suggested that he stay on in New York for one more year, arguing that he could learn more from him at the winery than he could at the university. Eric stayed on, putting his acceptance to Davis on hold for a year. Eric worked in the vineyards alongside his father and grandfather. Even as his grandfather encouraged him to stay, his father, Walter, encouraged him to leave, to go to California to complete his education so that he would have choices and options. Eric enjoyed going to work with his father every day, he enjoyed the work, the money was good for a young single guy and he felt there was always next year. Only after years had passed did Eric come to appreciate that his father and grandfather were both correct—the degree from Davis might have led to other opportunities, but the viticulture of California is not the viticulture of New York.[101] What he learned from his father and grandfather was more appropriate to the Finger Lakes than what he would have learned at Davis.

The shift toward *vinifera* was slow, but more acres were being planted. The peak of acres of vineyards in New York was reached in 1976. Since then, acreage has fallen off as juice and table grapes have met with increased competition from West Coast and offshore growers. Although native varieties were being ripped out or abandoned, more acres of *vinifera* and hybrids were being planted. In 1980, there were only 324 acres of *vinifera* reported in the entire state of New York.[102] By 1996, this would rise to more than 2,000 acres of Chardonnay, Riesling, Pinot Noir, Cabernet Sauvignon and other *vinifera* varieties, although this still represented less than 7 percent of the total grape production for the state.[103] In the 1980s, grape production began to stabilize at around 160,000 tons per year, and the overwhelming majority of the production remained in native varieties, even as the market for those grapes became more competitive and as the preferences of consumers continued to shift.

Throughout the 1970s, U.S. consumption of wine had grown dramatically, and preferences had been primarily for red wine; in 1970, 80 percent of the wine sold in the United States was red.[104] In the 1980s, wine consumption in the United States fell off a bit, but more importantly, preferences shifted from red to white wines. Although consumption declined, the dollar value of wine sales continued to increase as consumers selected more expensive wines. As more consumers moved away from the sweet wines and red wines, growers naturally planted more white wine varieties. In New York, the number of acres in the production of native varieties fell even as more acres of *vinifera* and hybrids were planted.

Through the early 1980s, more people began to publicly recognize Dr. Frank's contributions to the wine industry in the eastern United States. On May 26, 1980, Dr. Frank and Eugenia were host to thirty German viticultural scientists and grape growers who were visiting wineries in the United States. In addition to his current releases of wine, he provided a vertical tasting of his Riesling from 1969, 1972, 1974, 1975 and 1976. Before they left, they all signed an expression of their gratitude that said, in part, that they were "very impressed by the total typical and characteristic full Riesling wines with their fruity species [*sic*] aroma." Several years before, he had played host to about fifteen French grape growers and scientists who had come to see his vineyards and taste his wine. One of them remarked that he only hoped "Americans do not learn to appreciate these wines," signaling that he feared a loss of sales of imported French wine.

Unfortunately for the French growers, Americans *were* beginning to appreciate Konstantin's wine and other fine wines as well. The old belief that only imported wine was good wine had started to crumble under the quality of wines made in California and now in New York. Dr. Frank had always been a scientist and teacher first and not a businessman. Certainly he understood the need for sales and the attention to business, but his heart and mind were drawn to the lab and his ongoing experiments. He once told a reporter, "I am a scientist, not a businessman. You force me to sell my wine to support my scientific work. What I have here is a private research station that costs you not a penny. What do I need money for? Why should I die tomorrow and leave a million dollars?" The winery provided capital to fund his private research station, and to the extent that it did this, he was satisfied. He was growing more than sixty varieties of *vinifera* grapes and making small batches of wine from many of them. The scale was that of an experiment

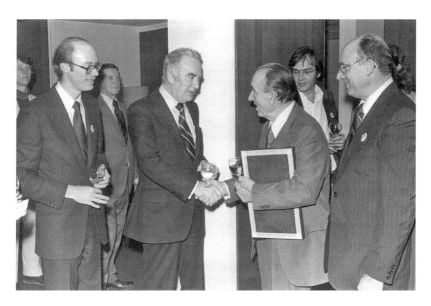

New York Department of Agriculture commissioner John Dyson, Governor Hugh Carey, Dr. Frank and Willy Frank on March 7, 1979, the occasion of Dr. Konstantin Frank Day in New York State.

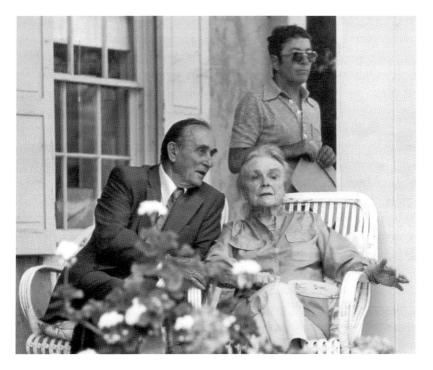

Dr. Frank and Elizabeth Furness, founder and owner of Piedmont Vineyards in Virginia, on the porch of her home in Virginia.

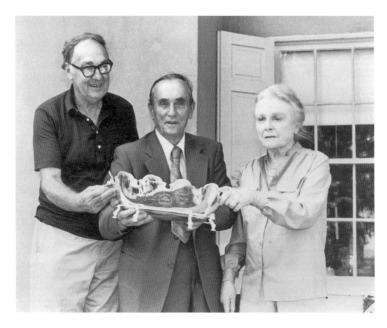

Robert de Treville Lawrence (left), Dr. Frank and Elizabeth Furness on the occasion of his being awarded the first Monteith Wine Bowl Trophy by the Atlantic Seaboard Wine Association.

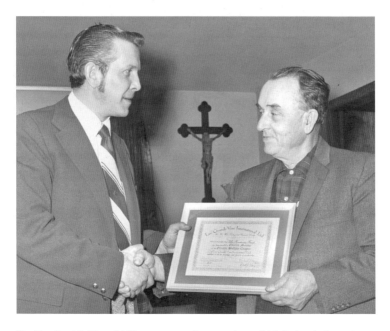

Dr. Frank with Donald Flanagan on the occasion of his being inducted as a charter member of the Les Grands Vins International Ltd. in Buffalo, New York.

station, not a winery business. People close to Dr. Frank and Willy have said that the older man resented what he believed was Willy's focus on profits and money. For Dr. Frank, the mission of the Vinifera Wine Cellars was primarily science and education, not profit.

On August 30, 1980, the Atlantic Seaboard Wine Association inaugurated the Monteith Trophy, to be presented each year to a person or organization making an outstanding contribution to the fields of viticulture or oenology. Originally organized as the Vinifera Wine Growers Association, the organization had evolved to be more inclusive and represent all growers of wine grapes. The inaugural award was given to Dr. Frank for "the lasting and unique contributions made to wine-growing and wine making…[which] qualified him above all others." The American Wine Society presented its

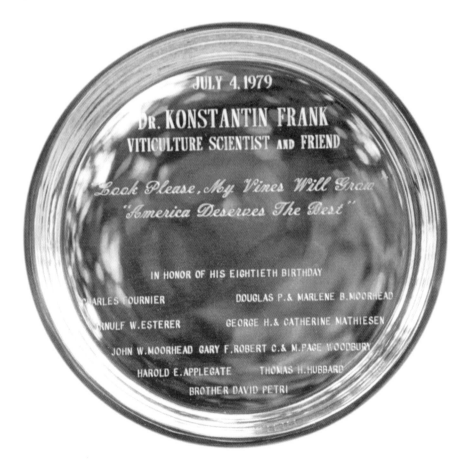

A silver plate given to Dr. Frank by his "cooperators" on the occasion of his eightieth birthday in 1979.

first-ever Award of Merit to Dr. Frank in 1981. By this time, at eighty-two years old, in addition to his other health problems, his eyesight was failing him, and he was suffering from the effects of diabetes. He no longer had the vigor for long days in the vineyard. He was also suffering from the signs of dementia. As a result, the quality of his work had been in decline for several years. Even old adversaries inquired after him. Charles Fournier responded to a letter from Philip Wagner in July 1982 saying, "He has not been in good health now for several years now but he seems to be able to get around and do some work. His vineyard has often looked ragged because part of his experimental plants is near the road."

Worse yet, as his health declined, so did the quality of his wine. He no longer took the extra efforts necessary to make excellent wine, he forgot to do things and he refused all help, and it showed up in the bottle. At the same time, sales suffered because his health prevented the long road trips that were required. Charles Fournier observed to Wagner, "I think his inventory is getting too big. He has transferred his company to his family, Willy is President—but he seems to be able to get around and do some work. Knows wine well, he's an excellent salesman but unfortunately his father hasn't let him do anything. Although he was willing to come and live here, he is remaining for the time being in New York and has kept his present job." As Konstantin's health continued to deteriorate, Willy could see the business collapsing around him. He tried to step in and help with winemaking, but his father would only have it his way. He continued to resent Willy's attempts to help and his suggestions about winemaking and continued to impose his order on the winery. He was to the end a teacher and a scientist and found the constant concern with business issues an unwanted distraction, and he continued to find Willy's interest in profits disdainful. Father and son fought bitterly over the business and its future. This was especially hard on Willy since he wanted to see his father's legacy preserved, and he desperately wanted his father's approval and recognition of his own contribution. It was not to be.

Once again, Dr. Frank asked Willy to come into the business full time, but only as a surrogate—not to make any changes or implement his own ideas. Konstantin wanted Fred, his grandson, to take over for him when the time came, and in spite of his health, that time was not here. For reasons known only to Dr. Frank, even now he did not want Willy to run the business. Willy demurred, not wanting to leave a successful sales career for an undefined role in the winery.

In the stress created between father and son and due to Konstantin's health, Walter Volz was left to fill the gap. In addition to managing the vineyards, Walter now was called on to take on a larger role in winemaking and managing the cellar. He worked to keep up the practices that he had mastered and the quality of the vineyards, but he was at home in the vineyard and working in the cellar; the actual winemaking and sales were not his first skills or interests. Furthermore, as Dr. Frank's health continued to decline, he would interfere with Walter's efforts and not cooperate. Attempts to work without him or to make decisions without him were unacceptable. Under very difficult circumstances, Walter did what he could to keep the business afloat. He found himself stuck between the powerful personalities of Dr. Frank and Willy. Over the years, Dr. Frank had alienated many of the local workers by shouting at them and generally subjecting them to what they thought of as mistreatment. Only through Walter's ongoing efforts to smooth out the rough patches and to insulate the workers from Dr. Frank were they able to find sufficient numbers of people for work crews. For a few

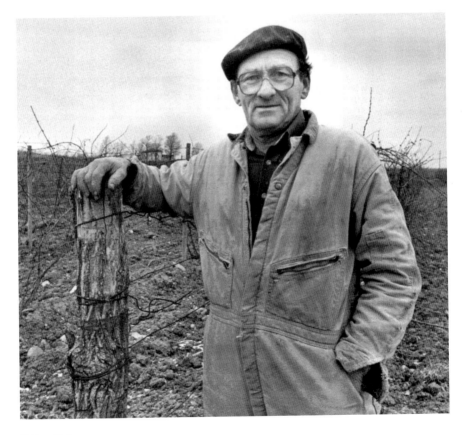

Walter Volz.

years in the early 1980s, the outlook at Vinifera Wine Cellars was beginning to look bleak. Dr. Frank still wanted to direct everything and make every decision, but he was no longer able to do so.

Friends and business associates tried to convince the old man that it was time for a change. It was time to bring Willy in as the manager of the winery. Thomas Abruzzini, a friend and distributor of Vinifera Wine Cellars in New York City, wrote an impassioned letter pleading for the good doctor to let Willy come in to the operation: "Just yesterday I received numerous copies of accolades and meritorious acclaim of your accomplishments in New York with the Vinifera grape variety and I thank you. In reading over all these copies, there is no doubt in my mind many years ago you did something no one dreamed of doing. This is the past but we are living in the present—the name of the game today is measured in SALES." He went on to describe the effort required for significant sales and the need to manage the inventory more closely and, finally, to say that "it will take a person like your son, Willy—if you give him a chance—leaving him COMPLETE CONTROL—and your PRESENCE at TASTINGS etc. etc. to start the sales rolling." Others provided counsel to the old man and encouraged him to let go of the operations.

CHATEAU FRANK

Willy, Margrit and the children continued to drive to the Finger Lakes most weekends, if not to work in their own vineyards then to work at Vinifera Wine Cellars. Eventually, they bought a stone house and wine cellar down the road from the winery that they eventually came to call the Chateau. The house was located on a slope roughly midpoint along the western side of Keuka Lake and had a panoramic view. It was built of local stone by a Mr. Speers for Philip Argus in 1886. Mr. Argus designed the home with a deep basement built into the side of the hill for the purpose of storing wine and fruit. At the same time the house was being constructed, he had another stone building constructed just behind it to be used for a pressing house. Argus had immigrated to the United States in 1855 and came to Hammondsport after living in Wisconsin for five years. He moved to Kansas in 1864 and lived there for eleven years trying to grow grapes. When he finally returned to the Finger Lakes in 1875, he bought and cleared the land and set out forty acres of grapes. He started the New York Wine Company making table wines from his own grapes. Eventually, the house and land

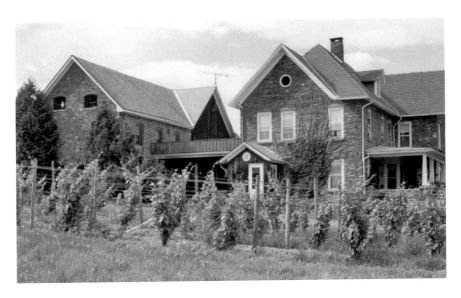

Chateau Frank.

were purchased by Greyton H. Taylor in 1969. Taylor, the president of the Taylor Wine Company, wanted to restore the property and start up a sparkling wine operation using grapes grown on the site. When he died in 1971, the property was left to his son, Walter Taylor, the founder and owner of Bully Hill Vineyards, located just up the hill.

Willy approached Walter Taylor about purchasing the property, and over the next few years, Walter would vacillate between wanting to sell and not wanting to sell. Greyton Taylor had long wanted to restore the old house to its earlier function and glory. Walter wavered between selling the place and completing his father's plans.[105] Finally, in 1982, a deal was reached, and the transaction took place. The Franks were particularly gratified to learn of the history of the house and the land—built by a German immigrant to be both home and winery as it was. They stayed in the house on weekends until they moved full time to the Finger Lakes in 1984.

Still, moving to the Finger Lakes from Long Island was heart-wrenching for the family. They had lived comfortably in a friendly neighborhood where they had many friends and an active social life. Willy's business as a manufacturer's representative had been successful and had grown to provide a good life. Margrit and Willy were able to travel widely and enjoy the fruits of success, and a move to the Finger Lakes would require them to give much of that up. Margrit Frank recalled crying as they left Long Island for the Finger Lakes. Today, Hammondsport, New York, is a pleasant village routinely described as "quaint," with well-kept nineteenth-century homes and an active picturesque village square. In the 1970s and early '80s, the village did not display the prosperity that it does today. Willy wrote to a friend that he was sorry for moving Margrit to the old cold stone house but that he felt it was something he had to do.[106] For her part, Margrit soon learned her way around and began to make new lifelong friends.

After they acquired the stone house, Willy and Margrit seriously thought about making sparkling wine in the traditional French fashion—the *methode champenoise*. People have speculated about his decision to make sparkling wine. Some have said that it was a way for Willy to distinguish himself without competing directly with his father and still win his approval. Others say that he was motivated because he thought there was a niche market for a boutique traditional sparkling wine. Margrit Frank agrees to this day that these may have been true but noted that his more practical motivation was, in part, to find a way to cover the taxes on the property. In any case, Willy went ahead with his plan. Traditional Champagne is a blend of usually three grapes: Pinot Noir, Chardonnay and Pinot Meunier, and so Willy planted those varieties on his farm. They called their sparkling wine venture Chateau Frank, and in the early years, they worked on the wines and business after hours at the Vinifera Wine Cellars. Everything was done by hand—riddling, disgorging and corking. Margrit Frank recalled that her job was to put the foil and wire cages on each finished bottle, twisting each cage in place by hand.

Dr. Frank was absolutely against the venture, declaring, "The only reason the French make champagne is because they can't make a decent table wine that far north." He told Willy that if he wanted a vineyard, there was already a family vineyard at Vinifera Wine Cellars. He was so set against Willy's venture that he refused to sell him vines from the Vinifera Wine Cellars nursery. Willy purchased the clones for his vineyards from other nurserymen.[107] Of course, Dr. Frank's observation about champagne was not entirely wrong. One of the challenges winemakers in the Champagne region of France face is a short and cool growing season—not unlike the Finger Lakes, Willy thought. The added sugar, brandy and second fermentation of the traditional Champagne method produced a sweet wine that would not have been possible otherwise. At the time the Champagne method was being perfected, sweeter wines were preferred, so most Champagnes of the time would have been much sweeter than the drier sparkling wines of today. Willy called his early releases Champagne, despite the fact that the French are notoriously protective of the term, insisting that only wines made in the region from grapes produced in the region can be called true Champagne.

The French government had negotiated legal protection for the use of the term in the 1891 Treaty of Madrid, which was the first international treaty created for the protection of trademarks. It reasserted this protection in the Treaty of Versailles, which ended World War I, making sure that the armistice included prohibitions against misuse of the term. Willy argued that the wines were made from the grape varieties of Champagne employing the method used in Champagne, so why not call it what it is? Eventually, he received attention from wine authorities in France and the European Union admonishing him for using the term but unable to do much else. Even the United States now bans the use of the term "Champagne" for all new U.S.-made wines, although all wines that were using the term before 2006 may continue to do so and then only when the name of the place of the wine's origin precedes it, as in "Finger Lakes Champagne." In the European Union, even the term *methode champenoise* is illegal when used outside the region, and other places producing sparkling wine must use the term *methode tradionnelle* instead.

Willy called his winery Chateau Frank and, like his father, aimed for the highest-quality product from the best possible grapes. His sparkling wines are estate wines made from grapes grown at Chateau Frank. Since he left his wine to rest for five to seven years, the first release from Chateau Frank, the 1985 vintage, was made in 1992. The natural process of producing a sparkling wine involves inducing a secondary fermentation. As the second fermentation takes place, the spent yeasts collect to form sediment. Allowing the wine to rest with these sediments in the bottle is said to allow the wine to develop its full flavor. In the traditional Champagne method, a bottle must rest on the lees for at least fifteen months for a non-vintage Champagne and three years for a vintage. Before the wine is sold, it is recorked to remove this sediment. This is done through a process called "riddling," where the bottles are stored upside down for a period of time and turned a quarter of a turn each day. This results in the sediment collecting near the cork. When the temporary cork is removed, the sediment is disgorged with a little bit of the wine, and then the bottle is topped off with the same vintage and a new cork quickly installed. One of the several reasons for the cost of good Champagne, and wine in general, is the fact that it is labor intensive; another is that inventories must be held for so long before the release.

It could easily be argued that Vinifera Wine Cellars had been more successful as a private experiment station than it had been as a business. Growing and vinifying so many varieties of grapes and not minding the cost of such an operation was not sustainable. Even in light of the changes already underway in the marketplace, Willy understood that his father's dream was slipping away. He could see that the operation was in desperate need of stronger management, but he was also aware of his father's single-mindedness, strong personality and reluctance to change. Even though he had been on the company letterhead since the beginning as an assistant director, his suggestions and ideas were routinely dismissed or ignored, not unlike his father's own experience when he first arrived in the Finger Lakes.

Konstantin could be a hard task master and a stubborn customer. At one point during a weekend trip some years earlier, Konstantin had poured Willy a glass of one of his red wines, and Willy had the temerity to offer a minor criticism. Dr. Frank walked away without a word and refused to pour his son another glass of red wine ever again.[108] Willy knew that he would have only one chance to establish the conditions for joining the business, and with a determination not unlike his father's, he relied on his own knowledge and focused on the outcomes. At the time, the business was in such poor shape financially that Willy was concerned that without significant change and effort, it would be forced to go into bankruptcy. As a result, the real equity value of the business was quite low. Willy approached his sisters with offers to buy some of their shares. Hilda and Walter Volz declined to sell, but Helene agreed to sell enough of her shares to allow Willy to have more than a 50 percent share in the business. With control firmly and legally in hand, he was prepared to finally join the business.

Part V

"WINES WORTHY OF THE GRAPES"

In 1984, Willy Frank took over operational control of Vinifera Wine Cellars and moved his family into the stone house up the road from the winery. Whereas Dr. Frank was always first a scientist and teacher, Willy Frank was a businessman and a salesman, and he found the condition of the business to be worse than even he feared. As his father's health and awareness had declined, the quality of the wine had suffered, the winemaking process was in disarray and cash flow was nearly nonexistent. Willy met with creditors and regulatory agencies to make arrangements and to buy some time. He found tanks of wine that had not been bottled and had turned nearly to vinegar, and many other barrels had spoiled as well. He sold off tanks of wine to vinegar companies to get rid of the product and generate cash. He sold more than twenty thousand gallons of wine in bulk to other wineries rather than sell it under the Vinifera Wine Cellars label.[109] He began to make visits to retail customers to assure them of continued operations and, in some cases, to try to recover their goodwill.

Although he was taking the necessary steps to save the winery and put the business back on a profitable footing, his father deeply resented his actions. Konstantin had long feared that Willy would be concerned only about profits and not quality, but Willy understood that without a solid business foundation, the winery could not last. Willy once told a reporter, "[My father] never considered this a business, I said, papa even the Catholic Church is a business—if there is no income, there is no church."[110] "I cleaned house," Willy said. "It hurt Papa but in the long run I believe it was better for our

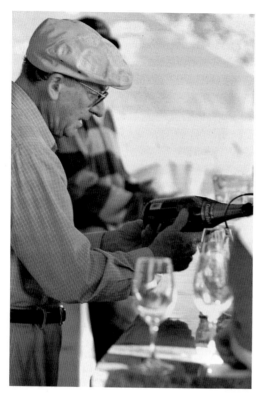

Willy Frank pouring a glass of Chateau Frank.

reputation." After decades of waiting to fully participate in the business, to bring his training and experience to bear on the problems and opportunities of the Vinifera Wine Cellars, he was finally in a position to act.

As Willy came on with a controlling interest and began to make changes, his brother-in-law, Walter Volz, may have felt marginalized; their relationship grew contentious. Although Willy and Walter consulted with each other on many of the decisions that needed to be made, Walter sometimes felt that Willy took full credit for many decisions that they had made together. When Willy spoke of the changes made to the business, he did not include the contribution or participation of Walter. Walter had come to the Finger Lakes in 1961, whereas Willy had not. He had worked with the old man every day since, while Willy had only showed up on occasional weekends, and when he did, there were always arguments and disagreements. As Dr. Frank's health had declined, Walter had slowly taken over as winemaker in addition to his responsibilities as vineyard manager. With his son, Eric, on board, the vineyards were well cared for, and he could focus more on winemaking.

Walter had envisioned more involvement in the business decisions, more consideration in charting the direction of the winery, but with Willy finally at the helm of the business, after waiting for twenty years, it was not to be. Walter knew the operations of the winery completely and did the work exactly as he was taught by Konstantin, but once in control, Willy was a force to be reckoned with and clearly in charge. Willy knew his limitations, though, and he knew that Walter and Eric were responsible for producing the quality and quantity of grapes that were the foundation that would eventually make Dr. Frank's

Vinifera Wine Cellars the most awarded winery in the eastern United States. He knew that they had maintained the quality of the vineyards even as other aspects of the business had declined. He also knew that to survive, the business had to be made profitable and that income would be generated by selling wine. For his part, Walter knew that Willy was clearly best suited to the task at hand, but Walter bristled at the scope of changes that were underway and his feelings of being marginalized. While Willy appreciated Walter's contribution, he saw himself as the last best hope for the business.

Although he had spent his life around vineyards and winemaking, Willy also knew he was not a winemaker and that a professional winemaker was needed to move the Vinifera Wine Cellars forward. He once noted that "winemaking was not given the same attention here that the vineyards were, and that's where I want to put my energies. We've got grapes of the greatest potential. Our job is to make wines worthy of the grapes." A professional winemaker was needed to pursue and maintain the quality of their wine. Of course, these decisions did not consider or recognize the contribution that Walter had been making to winemaking in the last ten years. Willy's decision to replace Walter was made unilaterally. Walter and Willy had heated and loud arguments during this transition, but Willy was now in charge and Walter had little leverage.

During the mid-1980s, there were no formal education opportunities for winemaking on the East Coast. The winemaking and viticulture programs were all in California. There had long been an expectation that Barbara Frank would someday be the winemaker at the Vinifera Wine Cellars, but at this time, she was still pursuing her education in California. At this time, winemaking in the few smaller wineries in New York was largely learned on the job or done by the winery owner; experience was gained over years and via informal internships and sharing of information. Local winemakers' experience was with native grapes and French hybrids; the experience with *vinifera* was limited to a few Europeans working at the large wineries like Gold Seal.

When Willy Frank stepped in to take over from his father, he was among the first of the new wineries to look outside the region and hire professional winemakers. As it happened, a young Californian named Mike Elliot was working at Glenora Wine Cellars at that time and was looking for an opportunity. He joined Vinifera Wine Cellars in 1984, excited to work with Dr. Frank and the *vinifera* grapes for a season before he and his wife returned to their native California. When Mike Elliot was working at Vinifera Wine Cellars, Dr. Frank was already suffering from poor health and Willy was running things, so Elliot had little meaningful interaction with Dr. Frank.[111]

The Maestro

Still in the market for a winemaker, Willy reached out to his father's old friend Andre Tchelistcheff to recommend another winemaker. Sometime during the 1960s, most likely at an industry event or perhaps on one of his trips to California while working for Gold Seal, Dr. Frank met Tchelistcheff, a fellow émigré from Russia. Tchelistcheff was born on December 7, 1901, near Moscow in what would become the Soviet Union. When he passed away in April 1994, he was widely recognized as the most influential post-Prohibition winemaker in the United States, especially in California. His family had been farmers for more than eight hundred years and had once held large tracts of land in Russia. His own father was a lawyer and a local judge.

Since Andre was unhealthy as a boy, he was tutored at home until he was about eleven years old. Although his father originally sided with the Bolsheviks in the 1917 revolution, his association with the czar and role in the existing government caused him to be viewed with some skepticism by the Bolsheviks. In 1918, he was declared an outlaw, and the family fled to the protection of the White Russian Army. Andre was studying in Paris but returned to join the White Army as a junior officer just in time to retreat through the Crimea to Gallipoli. He was captured and left for dead on the battlefield after the Bolsheviks machine-gunned a group of White Army prisoners. He fled to Yugoslavia, later studied agronomy at the University of Brno in Czechoslovakia and eventually studied winemaking and viticulture in France.

In 1938, he was hired by George de Latour of Beaulieu (BV) as vice-president and chief winemaker for the operations in California. De Latour founded Beaulieu in 1900 with the objective to bring world-class wine to the United States, and he desperately wanted to improve the quality of the post-Prohibition California wines. After Prohibition and the consolidation of wineries that followed, fine winemaking experience in California was in scant supply. Tchelistcheff had an almost immediate positive impact at Beaulieu in terms of improving the quality of wine. He became known as the "doctor" partially because of his habit of wearing white lab coats while in the winery but primarily because of his ability to identify and fix wines already in the barrel and to anticipate and solve problems before they were seen by others. He required a new standard of cleanliness in winemaking facilities and more carefully controlled and monitored production processes. He introduced innovations such as cold fermentation in California and the use of American oak barrels. His name was added to the Beaulieu Private

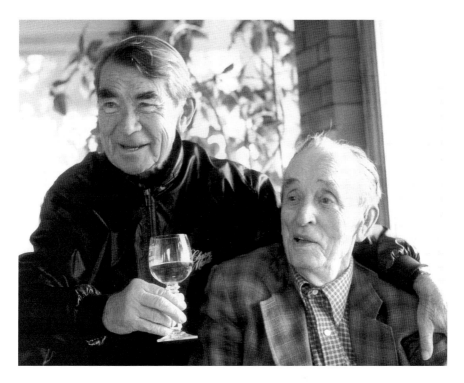

Andre Tchelistcheff and Dr. Frank.

Reserve label with the first vintage produced under his direction in 1940. In 1969, the Latour family sold Beaulieu, but Tchelistcheff never developed as strong a relationship with the new corporate owners as he had enjoyed with the Latour family. He retired from Beaulieu in 1973 and worked as an independent consultant to many wineries, including Robert Mondavi, Louis M. Martini, Franciscan Vineyards, Firestone, Jordan, Coppola, Buena Vista in California and others. He is often referred to as "the Maestro" and the "Father of California Winemaking."

Konstantin and Andre Tchelistcheff shared something of a common history and a passion for excellence in wine. When they would meet at an industry event, they would sit for hours drinking wine and talking in Russian. Both had fought for the White Army in the Bolshevik revolution. Both had left Russia as refugees and come to America to become renowned in the wine industry. One can only imagine what the two old Russian gentlemen would talk and laugh about in the corner of the room. Each made notable contributions to the development of the modern wine industry in the United States—Tchelistcheff in so many wineries in California and Dr. Frank as the father of the *vinifera* revolution in the East. Over the years, they had become close friends, and Tchelistcheff visited Konstantin in New York on several occasions. When Willy Frank decided in 1985 to bring a new professional winemaker on at Vinifera Wine Cellars, he turned to Tchelistcheff, who had only recently visited his old friend at the Vinifera Wine Cellars. Tchelistcheff recommended Eric Frey.

At the time, Eric Frey was working at Jordan Wines in Alexander Valley as an oenologist, and Andre Tchelistcheff was a consulting winemaker. Frey graduated from Indiana University with dual bachelor degrees in microbiology and psychology. After graduating, he went to work at Robert Mondavi's winery as a microbiologist. Mondavi was pleased with his work and sent him back to school to fill in a few academic gaps that would make him, as Frey says about himself, "a wine microbiologist."[112] Eventually, he traveled to Australia and to France to work and learn in other wineries and from other winemakers. He returned to the United States and was working at Jordan Wines as an oenologist when he spoke with Tchelistcheff about his desire to become lead winemaker somewhere. Tchelistcheff said, "Go see my old friend Konstantin Frank in New York." Frey questioned, "Why would I go to New York when I am already working in Napa and Sonoma?" "Go," Tchelistcheff said, "see the vineyards and the grapes. You can make good wine there."[113] By the time Eric Frey came on board in May 1985, Konstantin's health had deteriorated to such a degree that no meaningful interaction with him was possible. Willy was now running the winery, and Dr. Frank spent his days sitting on his porch. Frey recalled his first impression when he arrived at the winery was the sight of the "awesome vineyards."

THE FATHER OF *VINIFERA* IN THE EAST

In the last days of August 1985, at the age of eight-six, Dr. Frank suffered a stroke and was rushed to the hospital in Elmira. Over the next week, his condition grew worse. On September 6, 1985, he passed with members of his family gathered at his bedside. He is remembered throughout the United States as a pioneer and advocate for *vinifera* grapes and quality wine. Many people recalled him as an argumentative egotist and a combative self-promoter. His arguments claiming toxicity in French hybrids were remembered as self-serving and wrongheaded. Many others saw his strident efforts as necessary to push back the accepted wisdom and struggle to

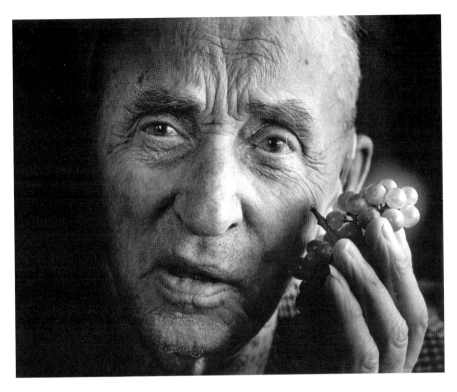

Dr. Konstantin Frank.

reveal the possibilities of a new sort of wine industry in the eastern United States. However, his obstinacy and confrontational manner may have been necessary for his success. He was known to say that he was "enthusiastic," a trait he valued as most important to his survival over the years.[114] Today, even more than twenty-five years after his death, questions about Dr. Frank are still able to provoke very strong reactions in people. Yet for every unflattering story, there are dozens of people who are excited to share their firsthand experiences with Dr. Frank with enthusiasm and heartfelt appreciation.

His reputation for combativeness and stubbornness is well deserved, but it is likely that a less forceful and committed person would not have been able to make the impact Dr. Frank did. The "go along to get along" culture of the agricultural authorities of his time saw no place for his ideas. Only Charles Fournier had the vision to see what was possible if *vinifera* could be grown in the East, but he lacked the expertise and knowledge to achieve that vision. With the support and resources of Fournier, Dr. Frank brought his knowledge to literally bear fruit and then went on to champion *Vitis vinifera* to all who would listen and even some who would not. The change he brought to the wine industry in the eastern United States in such a short time was accomplished by the force of his personality as much as by the power of his ideas.

In the brief twenty years or so since he released the first vintage of wine from his Vinifera Wine Cellars, he had received accolades from four governors of New York and had been honored with "Dr. Konstantin Frank Day" by Governor Hugh Carey. In the end, there was at least one thing on which Governors Nelson Rockefeller, Hugh Carey and Mario Cuomo agreed. A lengthy recognition and appreciation was read into the *Congressional Record* by his congressman, and he received many honors and awards. His wines were served on a number of occasions at the White House, as well as for the visiting queen of England. Dr. Frank's wine was served at the Wye River Conference between President Bill Clinton and Boris Yeltsin. The story is told that the two leaders talked well into the night and sent out for more wine several times.

When Dr. Frank passed away, eulogies appeared throughout the United States praising his work and remembering his struggle. Although some acrimony still existed, at the end of his life, there was no doubt about his impact and success. As word of his passing spread across the industry internationally, some in the Russian wine industry contacted friends in the United States to learn more about this man they were reading about in the business papers and journals. As a "nonperson," all traces of Konstantin Frank and his family had been removed from the Soviet institutions. People in Ukraine read about him and his importance to wine in the United States but found few traces of him in his homeland.

There is something to "nonperson" status in the United States as well. Even as late as 1986, the experiment station in Geneva was unable or unwilling to give credit where the credit was clearly due. In an article in the *New York Food and Life Science Quarterly* in early 1985, a staff member wrote, "Since colonial times New York vineyardists have tried strenuously but unsuccessfully to grow European or *Vitis vinifera* grape varieties which are unsurpassed in quality for wine production. In a large part because of research conducted at the Geneva Agricultural Experiment Station these efforts are finally resulting in commercial success." Not a word or a nod to Dr. Frank or Charles Fournier, no acknowledgement of the station's role in delaying progress. Willy Frank fired off a letter asking where this groundbreaking research was and, more to the point, where it was currently. He pointedly asked why the station was still doing so little *vinifera* research when there was clearly such a significant opportunity. He also asked them to please avoid trying to rewrite history in the future.

When the 1976 Farm Winery Act passed, there were 19 wineries in New York, including the largest, such as Taylor and Gold Seal. As this is being written in 2014, there are more than 350 wineries, the overwhelming majority of which are small "farm" operations as defined by the act. According to the National Agricultural Survey and the New York State Fruit Tree and Vineyard Survey, the number of acres of native grape varieties is generally declining thoughout the state even as more acres of *Vitis vinifera* are

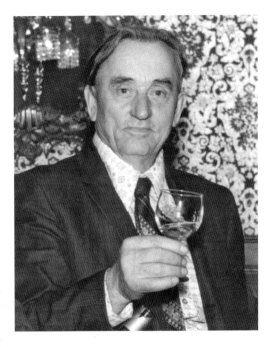

Dr. Frank. Cheers!

planted. *Vinifera* grapes are successfully cultivated and wines are produced in no fewer than fifteen states of the eastern United States. Suffice it to say, the success of Vinifera Wine Cellars and that of the other *vinifera* growers and wine producers in the eastern United States stands in part as testimony to the strength of Konstantin Frank's ideas, his passion and his vision.

Dr. Frank was also an ardent patriot and enthusiast for all things American. His experience under the Soviet system had made him distrustful of the Soviets and wary of their intentions. He would not let his house be photographed unless the flag was flying from the tall flagstaff in his yard, and he was extremely proud of his citizenship. He told many people over the years, "You do not appreciate what a great country this is like I do." He saw the history of *Vitis vinifera*, from Thomas Jefferson and other early innovators, as a single thread leading to his own success and, eventually, to a cultural redefinition—an American tradition of fine wine. He foresaw *vinifera* growing in twenty or more states and excellence in winemaking throughout the land. This was the vision he saw when he claimed in 1958 to have started the "second American Revolution." For these accomplishments, he is known as the "Father of *Vinifera* in the East."

The Rise of Eastern Wine

With the passing of "Papa," Willy Frank was now clearly the leader of the Vinifera Wine Cellars and his father's legacy. Willibald Karl Frank was a MBA graduate from the University of Nuremberg and a successful salesman. He had a strong business acumen that he brought to the winery, which included an appreciation for marketing and developing a brand. He would need those skills to turn the Vinifera Wine Cellars into a viable business. In the early 1980s, the interest in fine wine had continued to drive retail and restaurant sales to ever higher amounts in dollars and volume. But as the decade went on, and just as Willy took over operational control of the Vinifera Wine Cellars, this interest seemed to cool a bit.

Throughout the late 1980s, because of public warnings of the health risks associated with alcohol in general and sulfites in wine in particular, coupled with greater attention being given to driving under the influence, wine consumption began to fall off in the United States. At the same time, more states began to raise legal drinking ages and pass stricter laws pertaining to DUI. When he moved his family to the Finger Lakes and acquired a controlling interest in the Vinifera Wine Cellars, Willy started to put the business on a sustainable footing. Even as he started his work, the market itself began to tighten as sales across the industry declined. Initial steps meant to increase cash flow and clear out poor-quality inventory helped, but if the business were to reach its potential, Willy understood that more attention was needed in the winemaking process and wine sales. So, after the first steps were taken to move the business toward profitability, Willy also took some steps to solidify the Dr. Frank Vinifera Wine Cellars brand. He had the wine labels redesigned to a modern appearance highlighting the winery's scenic location above Keuka Lake. And he took the steps to purchase French oak barrels to age the wine to replace the American oak barrels on which his father had insisted.

Willy Frank became a tireless representative of the wines of the Vinifera Wine Cellars, in particular, but also a self-appointed spokesman and champion of eastern *vinifera* wines in general. Like his father had done in the 1960s and '70s, Willy hit the road. Instead of academic presentations and lectures, he was interested in selling wine, but he also was selling Finger Lakes wine writ large. Willy knew that a rising tide lifts all boats, so what was good for Finger Lakes wine in general was good for Dr. Frank's Vinifera Wine Cellars, too. His affable manner and passion affected nearly everyone who met him. Still, where Dr. Frank's growth and reputation had been

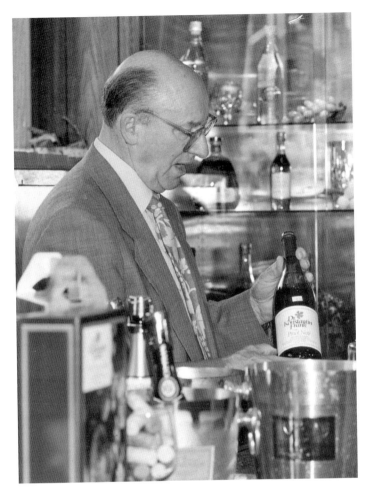

Willy Frank promoting Dr. Frank's wines.

made in an expanding market, Willy's work was started in a contracting market. In addition, there were still lingering doubts about the quality of New York State wine.

When Eric Frey first came to Keuka Lake, he was most impressed by the condition of the vineyards and the quality of the grapes, as well as with Walter Volz, the vineyard manager. Volz, Frank's son-in-law and longtime vineyard manager, had learned to maintain the highest standards of quality in the vineyards, which, in turn, produced very high-quality grapes. Frey recalled making some very good wines while at the Vinifera Wine Cellars and credited the quality of the wine to the character and

137

quality of the grapes being grown by Walter Volz; his son, Eric Volz, would tell him that the decisions made in the vineyard are revealed in the bottle—always quality first.

Dr. Frank's mantra of excellence was inculcated in everyone who worked with him, and Walter Volz brought this knowledge to bear on every vine under his care. The soils at the Vinifera Wine Cellars are prone to erosion, and protecting the thin topsoil is a critical element in managing the vineyards. Dr. Frank's and eventually Walter and Eric Volz's management of the vineyards is remarkable not only for the success of the *vinifera* they grew but also for the soil conservation and management practices that have made the operation a continued success for more than fifty years. Winemakers agree that wine quality begins in the vineyard and that, at its heart, the wine business is farming. Every winemaker interviewed for this book who worked for the Vinifera Wine Cellars made a point of praising the quality of the vineyards and the work of Walter and Eric Volz as the critical element in Dr. Frank's wines.

Dr. Frank's health was so poor when Eric Frey arrived at the winery that he was confined to the porch and the house for the most part. Frey did not recall ever having so much as a conversation with him. Willy was struggling to pump life back into the moribund business. While he was

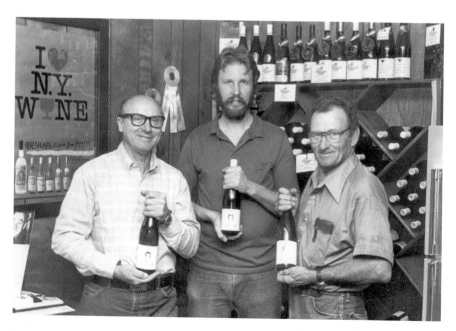

Willy Frank, Eric Frey and Walter Volz.

involved in key decisions, he let Frey do what he was hired to do: make wine. Frey was pleased to discover that Dr. Frank was also growing so many varieties of grapes that, as winemaker, he was able to work with many different grapes and wines, some he had not even heard of before coming to New York from California.

Less exciting was the condition of the winemaking operation itself. Dr. Frank had mastered the art of repurposing and reusing not just equipment but also parts and pieces of equipment. The winery was built for small volumes of production; the larger volumes needed for commercial success were not envisioned. All in all, the frugality had saved money when saving money was important, but it had led to a messy, difficult-to-manage operation as the winery grew. Of course, given the financial condition of the winery, they did not have the capital for items like new tanks, new pipes and rewiring the winery. So, changes were made as needed, and plans began to be drawn up for more exhaustive upgrades.

Slowly the winery began to take shape, but money remained in short supply. Willy and Walter took no salaries during this period. As difficult as the circumstances were, though, Eric Frey began to make some very good wine. With improved product, Willy had something to take to the customers and to the public. They began to enter wine competitions and win recognition—occasionally against better-known California wines and even European wines. With recognition once again came reporters and news stories. Dr. Frank had learned the power of the press and self-promotion, and Willy leveraged his father's reputation for still more publicity and attention.

After about five successful years, Eric Frey was recruited away to join the Lenz Winery on Long Island in the spring of 1989. When he left, Willy contacted Barbara Frank and asked her to return from California to assume the role of head winemaker at both the Vinifera Wine Cellars and Chateau Frank. Barbara had finished her education and specialized in making sparkling wine. When Willy called for her to come back to the family wine business, she was assistant winemaker at S. Anderson. She returned to take over winemaking operations at Dr. Frank's just as the 1989 harvest approached. She reached out to her friend and colleague from California, Mark Veraguth, to come east for a couple of months to help.

Barbara and Mark had become friends when they both worked at S. Anderson while she was in school in California. Mark had been born and raised in Napa Valley and started working on the S. Anderson Winery while still in high school. He would return to the winery each summer through college, working his way up from field labor to cellar work and assisting in winemaking. While at the

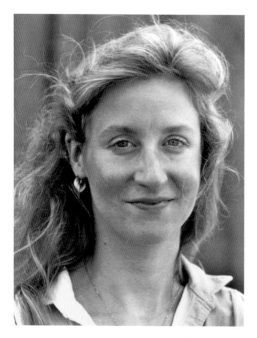

Barbara Frank.

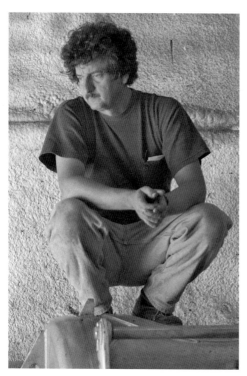

University of California–Davis, he majored in civil engineering but took additional chemistry and winemaking classes as electives. When he graduated from UC–Davis, the Andersons offered him an opportunity to stay on as an assistant winemaker. He accepted. While at S. Anderson, he also met and worked with Andre Tchelistcheff, who was consulting with the Andersons at the time. Tchelistcheff used to call him his "little engineer."[115]

Mark's value as a winemaker was underscored by his value as an engineer. He surveyed the winery composed of repurposed dairy equipment, truck tanks fitted to serve in the winery operations, snaking hoses through holes punched in walls and pumps and hoses running up and down stairs. He saw that the electrical wiring issues and the makeshift equipment were built to save money in the early days but knew they were cumbersome and often dangerous to use. As soon as the crush was over, Mark set about addressing what he saw as the most serious issues in the winery. His task of upgrading and retrofitting would keep him busy for years to come.[116]

Left: Mark Veraguth.

140

With Barbara, Mark Veraguth and Walter and Eric Volz, Willy felt confident that he had a team in place for the long haul, and he could focus his attention on sales and the Vinifera Wine Cellars brand. Early in the spring of 1990, Barbara suffered injuries in a car accident that precluded her from continuing the physical demands required of a head winemaker. After less than a year with the winery, she moved to Westchester, New York, to focus on her teaching skills and study sales and marketing at the International Wine Center in New York City. She eventually began to work in the family business as a regional sales representative in the metropolitan region. Throughout this period and to the present, she continued as a consulting winemaker for the Chateau Frank sparkling wines.[117]

Without a head winemaker once again, Willy started another search. At the time, Peter Bell was working in New Zealand as a winemaker but was ready for a change when a friend suggested he look into the Finger Lakes. His friend explained that something was ready to happen to wine in the Finger Lakes and that Peter might find an opportunity there. Not knowing anything about the Finger Lakes region, much less Finger Lakes wine, he looked up some wineries there. He contacted Taylor Wine but was told that Taylor was about to enter bankruptcy and had no need for a winemaker. He did learn from that contact that Dr. Frank's Vinifera Wine Cellars was in the market for a winemaker, and so Peter contacted Willy. He was exactly what Willy needed at the time. Willy invited Peter to visit, and while he was there, he loaned him a car so he could look around the area for himself. They tasted wine from the Eric Frey years, and at some point, Willy made Peter an offer to be head winemaker. So, Peter Bell moved his wife and young children from New Zealand to Hammondsport and took up the responsibilities of head winemaker. He arrived in August 1990 to begin his work. As Mark Veraguth continued to upgrade and replace and repair equipment, Peter went to work, slowly bringing the winery operations up to the modern standards to which he was accustomed.

For many people, Willy Frank became the face of New York wine as much as the president of Dr. Frank's Vinifera Wine Cellars. He traveled up and down the East Coast much like his father had been doing since the 1960s. Where Konstantin was a missionary selling *vinifera* and good wine, Willy was promoting all New York wine, although Dr. Frank's Vinifera Wine Cellars and *vinifera* wines always came first. As Willy's cachet as a wine personality began to grow, staff at the Vinifera Wine Cellars were frequently dismayed to hear Willy tell visitors that the winery was a one-man operation—he seemed to take credit for work done by others in the operation. This became

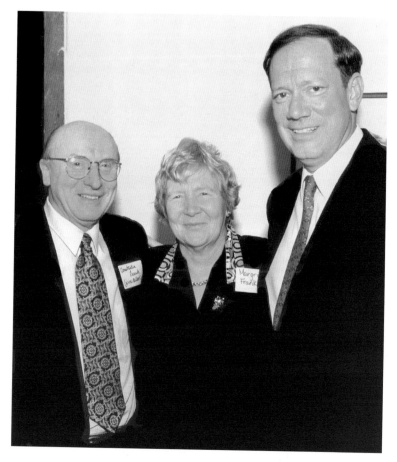

Willy and Margrit Frank with New York governor George Pataki.

increasingly difficult for Walter Volz, and the frequency and intensity of the arguments between Walter and Willy grew; as a result, the degree of internal drama at the Vinifera Wine Cellars was soon as great as ever. At the same time, Willy's efforts to improve sales and market the Dr. Frank brand were paying off.

In 1993, Willy experienced some serious health problems and called on his son, Fred, to finally join the business. Fred Frank joined the family business as president, with Willy becoming chairman of the board. Willy recovered from his illness faster and more completely than was feared. Now that Fred was on board, he would run the business operations, and a restored Willy would be free to truly direct sales and marketing. Fred brought the experience of Banfi, the largest importer of wine to the

United States at the time, to bear on the operations and began to make some of his own changes to operations. Many of Fred's changes and suggestions were challenged by his father. They would argue, and as the temperature of the disagreement would rise, the argument would shift from English to German. But Fred's disposition was such that he would simply wait for the circumstances to change or time to pass to make his presence felt on the organization. This non-confrontational approach may have slowed Fred's influence in those early days, but it also reduced the emotional intensity in the operations. Slowly, over the next few years, Fred asserted full control over operations.

The tension with Willy reached a level of complete exasperation for Walter at about this time. With the changes occurring in operations and the sense of being passed over in the business and the legacy, Walter made the decision to leave the winery that he had helped build and the vineyards he had planted and maintained with Dr. Frank for about thirty years. Land adjacent to the vineyard had come up for sale in the early '90s, and Willy and Walter each approached the owner about purchasing it. Eventually, Walter purchased the fourteen-acre parcel. At last he had his own vineyard, a place where he would decide when to work, what to grow and how to grow it. In 1994, he retired from Vinifera Wine Cellars and set to work in his own vineyard. With Walter's retirement, his son, Eric, stepped in to fill his shoes and became the vineyard manager. Of course, Eric had learned his craft from Dr. Frank himself and from his father over nearly twenty years of day-to-day and head-to-head work. The vineyards remained in good hands, but an important era of the Vinifera Wine Cellars had passed.

Salmon Run

Fred Frank brought a good deal of experience from his time with Banfi. Once on board as president, though, he recognized that Dr. Frank's best wines would always be limited in quantity by virtue of the limited volume of estate grapes they were able to grow. By the 1990s, many of the vines on the original vineyard were already more than forty years old and needed to be replaced. Some of the oldest *vinifera* vines in production in the United States were to be found in Dr. Frank's vineyards. Older vines are known to produce better wine but fewer grapes. As these vines continued to age, the best Vinifera Wine Cellars wines would be made from these old vines (and they

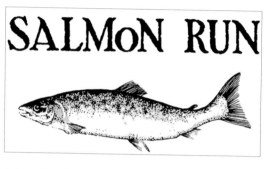

Salmon Run label.

would continue to improve as time passed), but they were limited in quantity. To survive as a business, Vinifera Wine Cellars needed to produce greater volumes of good wine. Expanding the vineyards was necessary, but the quality of the premium wine could not be sacrificed. Fred proposed a line of wines made in the same methods and by the same winemakers but made with grapes from younger vines or purchased grapes to fill the gap in the Vinifera Wine Cellars' offerings. The Salmon Run line, named after the landlocked salmon found in Keuka Lake, was founded in 1993. Its first release was made in 1994 by Peter Bell and Mark Veraguth. Today, Salmon Run represents about half of the winery's total sales.

Eventually, Peter Bell left the Vinifera Wine Cellars for a position as winemaker with Fox Run Vineyards on Seneca Lake, and Fred Frank found himself in the position of once again looking for a winemaker. Over the next few years, a number of talented winemakers came and went from the Vinifera Wine Cellars, drawn to new opportunities elsewhere. David Munksgard succeeded Peter Bell, and within a year or two, Dana Keeler joined to replace Munksgard. Keeler left after two more years. In February 1999, Willy interviewed Morten Hallgren, who had been working as a winemaker at the Biltmore Estates Winery in North Carolina. The interview turned into a hands-on experience, as Morten became immediately involved in some issues in the winery. This led to being hired as head winemaker, a position he held from March 1999 until May 2004, when he left to run his own Ravines Winery.

The experience of losing winemakers at such a steady pace was a critical concern for the operation. It was clear that winemakers would leave as new opportunities became open to them; with the growth in the industry, there would continue to be new opportunities. To mitigate the impact of the revolving door in the winemaking operation, a management approach was developed that involved having multiple winemakers from around the world come to work at the Vinifera Wine Cellars for a time. Morten Hallgren took on the responsibility as first among equals, managing multiple interns and winemakers. Rather than a committee approach, each winemaker assumed

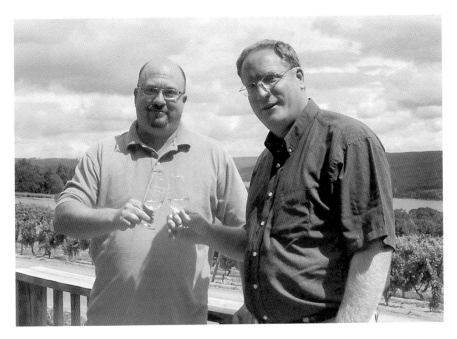

Eric Volz and Fred Frank (right) celebrating the fiftieth anniversary of Dr. Frank's Vinifera Wine Cellars.

the responsibilities for the varietal or type of wine he knew best—in principle, at least. Where Willy had focused the wine list on fewer wines, the wine list had grown once again as customer tastes changed and wine drinkers became willing to enjoy a wider range of wines. The team approach has paid off—with winemaking expertise drawn from around the world, everyone learns and the wine benefits the most, with each variety receiving the appropriate attention and technique. It has also benefited winemaking in the Finger Lakes in general, as many of the visiting winemakers and interns have gone on to other wineries. The influx of professionally trained winemakers passing through Dr. Frank's has likely had a marked impact on the quality of wine made in the Finger Lakes and beyond.

This strategy has also contributed to Dr. Frank's Vinifera Wine Cellars ranking as the New York State winery with the most awards from competitions. The wine competitions are taken seriously because wines are selected by judges blindly, not knowing whose wine they are tasting. As such, in Fred Frank's view, at least, they are as objective a measure of quality as one can hope for. In 2013, Dr. Frank's Vinifera Wine Cellars earned 129 gold medals in national and international wine competitions,

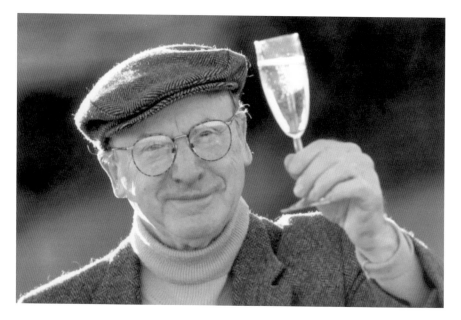

Willy Frank. Cheers!

a record for a New York winery. Experience matters as well. Mark Veraguth heads up the winemaking team and has been with Dr. Frank's since 1989, and he remains the institutional memory of winemaking operations. Other members of the current winemaking team include Eric Bauman, the sparkling winemaker at Chateau Frank. Eric is from Rochester, New York, and joined the winery in 2005 after eight years at J Winery in Sonoma, California, learning to produce premium sparkling wine. Peter Weis is a German winemaking specialist and has been with the winery for six years. He grew up on a Mosel vineyard in Germany and attended the Bad Kreuznach Technical School for Winemaking in that country. Jonathon Luestner attended winemaking school at the University of Adelaide in Australia and worked at several Australian wineries prior to joining Dr. Frank's in 2009.

In 2000, Willy Frank was awarded the Monteith Wine Bowl Trophy by the Atlantic Seaboard Wine Association, twenty years after his father received the same recognition. The award is "presented to individuals or organizations that have performed exceptional contributions to the development and sustainability of the American wine industry by actively providing leadership and motivation in addressing both legislative and regulatory issues that confront the industry, supporting innovative and technical research in both the fields of enology and viticulture, also encouraging wine and health related studies, as well as contributing to consumer public wine education and appreciation through the arts, literature and the public media."[118]

As time passed, Willy and Margrit began to spend winters in Florida, where Willy would make sales calls on local restaurants and distributors while supposedly relaxing. Even on his vacations, he would travel around Florida for wine shows and sales calls. In March 2006, while on a sales trip to Florida, Willy Frank passed away at his home in Bonita Springs, at the age of eighty. At the time of his passing, the wines from Dr. Frank's Vinifera Wine Cellars were being sold in thirty states, believed to be more than any other premium New York State winery.

Celebration

In 2012, Dr. Frank's Vinifera Wine Cellars celebrated the fiftieth anniversary of its first release. The event was marked by a gathering of invited guests, longtime friends and enthusiastic supporters. It was also marked by the winery

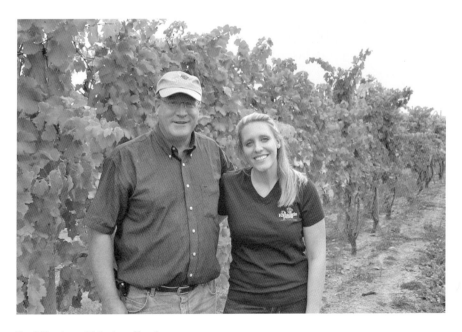

Fred Frank and Meghan Frank.

winning more awards than any other year and being named Winery of the Year by New York State for the third time. Over the years, Vinifera Wine Cellars has received national and international recognition. The success of *vinifera* is testimony to the vision and work of Dr. Konstantin Frank and members of the Frank family. The growth of small wineries is the result of changing tastes and public policy, but the place of *vinifera* in those wineries also rests as part of the same vision. Early adopters and cooperators took risks, often against the advice of experts, to try something new based in varying degrees on the enthusiasm and demonstrations of Dr. Frank. The vision of a family estate winery figured prominently in Konstantin's dream, and he lived to see his grandsons working in the business. In 2013, Meghan Frank, the fourth generation of the family, joined the business, cementing another step in the dream of Konstantin Frank.

NOTES

PART I

1. George S. Conover, ed., "History of Business in Geneva, New York," *History of Ontario County New York*, comp. Lewis Cass Aldridge (Syracuse, NY: D. Mason & Company, 1893), http://history.rays-place.com/ny/geneva-9.htm.
2. Ibid.
3. Cornell University College of Agriculture and Life Sciences, New York State Agricultural Experiment Station, "History of the Experiment Station," http://www.nysaes.cornell.edu/cals/nysaes/about/history.cfm.
4. Interview with Dr. Konstantin Frank by Hudson Cattell, September 1975.
5. Joseph Height, PhD, *Paradise on the Steppes*, 4th ed. (Chelsea, MI: Book Crafters, 1973), 17–22.
6. Genealogical research by Robert W. Hutton, from a letter written to Willy and Frederick Frank on December 20, 2000, from Mr. Hutton.
7. Genealogical research by author; various online sources.
8. Much of the history of the Frank family has been reconstructed by the author using online resources and documentation provided by the Frank family.
9. Fred LeBrun, "New York State's Genius Grape Grower," *Albany (NY) Sunday Times Union*, October 19, 1990.
10. Wikipedia, "History of Germans in Russia and the Soviet Union," http://en.wikipedia.org/wiki/History_of_Germans_in_Russia_and_the_Soviet_Union.
11. Interview with Lena Schelling.

12. Dr. Konstantin Frank, *Curriculum Vitae*, 1952. From Dr. Frank's personal papers, provided by the Frank family.

13. Frank résumé written to Geneva Experiment Station.

14. Ibid.

15. Conversation with Lena Schelling, June 2011.

16. Papers of Dr. Konstantin Frank, translated by Robert Hutton.

17. Interview with Robert Hutton, July 2011.

18. From notes written by Dr. Frank on photos from the time.

19. Discussion with Olga Shaposhnikova, June 4, 2011.

20. Dr. Frank résumé.

21. Wikipedia, "Treaty of Non-Aggression between Germany and the Soviet Union," http://en.wikipedia.org/wiki/Treaty_of_Non-Aggression_between_Germany_and_the_Soviet_Union.

22. Interviews with Helene Schelling, June 5 and October 7, 2011.

23. Wikipedia, "Andrey Vlasov," http://en.wikipedia.org/wiki/Andrey_Vlasov.

24. Interview with Helene Schelling, October 2011.

25. Interview with Robert Hutton, July 2011.

26. Conversation with Lena Schelling, June 2011.

27. Interview with Margrit Frank, July 2011; interview with Lena Schelling, June 2011.

28. Ibid.

29. Interviews with Margrit Frank, Lena Schelling and Fred Frank.

30. At the end of the war, many countries agreed to accept displaced persons and refugees from Europe. Many nations of South America already had substantial populations of German immigrants and were willing to accept more. Georges Frank accepted free transportation to Argentina under one of the Red Cross programs that assisted displaced people. This information was collected in interviews with Lena Schelling and from a newspaper article from Bath, New York, at the time Georges visited Konstantin in New York. *The Leader*, August 23, 1961.

31. Displaced Persons' Camp, "Repatriation of Ukrainian Displaced People After World War II," http://www.dpcamps.org/repatriation.html.

32. North American Immigration, "Displaced Persons Act (United States) (1948)," http://immigration-online.org/86-displaced-persons-act-united-states-1948.html.

33. From an interview with Helene Schelling.

34. Interviews with Margrit Frank and Helene Schelling.

35. USNS *Blatchford* ship's manifest.

36. From a publication prepared on board the USNS *Blatchford* by the Immigrant Refugee Organization for the passengers.

37. Interview with Helene Schelling, June 2011.

38. Ibid.

39. Dr. Konstantin Frank, *Curriculum Vitae*, 1952.

40. In the May 1952 edition of the Geneva Experimental Station newsletter, Dr. Frank was presented as a new employee working on a grant with Dr. Karl Brase. Dr. Brase was born and educated in Germany.

Part II

41. Geneva Station newsletter (April 1952).

42. Cornell University eCommons, "Karl Dietrich Brase," http://ecommons. cornell.edu/bitstream/1813/18189/1/Brase_Karl_Dietrich_1966.pdf.

43. From a letter written by Dr. Frank to Harold F. Winters and William Ackerman at the United States Department of Agriculture, Agricultural Research Service, July 20, 1973.

44. Concord Grape Juice, "Grape Growing in New York," http://www. concordgrapejuice.com/growinghistory.htm.

45. Professional Friends of Wine, "Wine History," February 13, 2012, http://www.winepros.org/wine101/history.htm.

46. Kate Whitesell, "The Lake Effect on the Surrounding Climate of the Finger Lakes in New York," Keck Geology Consortium, http:// keckgeology.org/files/pdf/symvol/18th/fingerlakes/whitesell.pdf.

47. Hudson Cattell, "The Pioneering Years at Brights," *Wines East* (July– August 1986).

48. *Wines East*, "Centennial in Geneva, New York" (July–August 1982).

49. Found in the New York State Agricultural Experiment Station library.

50. Konstantin Frank, "The Present Vista for the Vitis Vinifera European Grape Varieties in the East," unpublished notes from the Dr. Frank Archive.

51. Attributed to Dr. Frank in an interview with Fred Frank, July 2010.

52. Interviews with Lena Schelling, Margrit Frank and Darmon Gleason.

53. Interview with Darmon Gleason, July 2010.

54. Frank Prial, "Wine Talk," *New York Times*, July 13, 1983.

55. In Dr. Frank's notes for the article "The Present Vista for the Vitis Vinifera European Grape Varieties in the East." These remarks were not included in the final form of the article.

56. Frank, "Present Vista for the Vitis Vinifera," 12.

57. Ibid., 15.

58. Field notes of T.W. Markham, county agricultural agent, August 1960. From Dr. Frank's personal papers, provided by the Frank family.

59. Frank, "Present Vista for the Vitis Vinifera," 15.

60. Charles Fournier, "A Scientific Look at Vinifera in the East," *Wines & Vines* 42, no. 8 (August 1961).

61. Letter from Philip Wagner to Charles Fournier, September 24, 1958, Wagner letters, Cornell University Library archive.
62. Ibid.
63. Prial, "Wine Talk."
64. Interview with Fred Frank, April 2011.
65. Interview with Darmon Gleason, July 2011.
66. Interview with Helen Schelling, June 2011.
67. Photos from this period of volunteers working with the Franks planting vines include references of individuals being from the Geneva station.
68. As quoted in G.H. Mowbray, "The Eclectric Wine Taster," *American Wine Society Journal.*
69. Interview with Darmon Gleason, July 2010.

PART III

70. Interview with Margit Frank, 2010.
71. Interview with Helene Schelling, 2010.
72. Interview with Margrit Frank, 2010.
73. Interview with Eric Volz, 2011.
74. Ibid.; interview with Margrit Frank, 2010.
75. Interview with Eric Frey, June 2010.
76. Interview with Eric Volz, 2011; interview with Eric Frey, 2011.
77. These notarized statements still exist in the Frank family archive and were viewed by the author as part of the research for this book.
78. William Clifford, "New York Wines Come of Age," *Holiday* (May 1968).
79. Interview with Eric Volz, 2010; Konstantin Frank, "Early Experiments: Vinifera Wine Cellars," *Vinifera Wine Growers Journal* (Winter 1979).
80. Wine Institute, "Wine Consumption in the U.S.," http://www.wineinstitute. org/resources/statistics/article86; New York Wines, "Economic Impact of New York State Grapes, Grape Juice and Wine," 2005, http://www. newyorkwines.org/resources/1e2397ca92f7422da876d0c948ff45cf.pdf.
81. Pennsylvania Wine Marketing and Research Program, a joint venture of GLOBAL WINE PARTNERS US LLC, Frank, Rimerman + Co. LLP CPAs copyright ©2006 by MKF Research LLC, the Wine Business Center, 899 Adams Street, Suite E, St. Helena, California, 94574, (707) 963-9222, www.mkfresearch.com.
82. M.A. Amerine and M.A. Joslyn, *Table Wines: The Technology of Their Production,* 2nd ed. (Berkeley: University of California Press, 1970), 267. Available on GoogleBooks.
83. Letter from M.J. Ryan, Acting Director, Office of Legislative Services, United States Department of Health, Education and Welfare, June 23, 1970.

84. From a letter written by Philip Wagner to Charles Fournier, November 5, 1963.

85. From a letter from Dr. Frank to Harry L. Showalter, March 30, 1971.

86. Frank, "Early Experiments."

87. Ruth Ellen, "Dr. Frank Best Described as Worker, Dreamer, Realist," *Chicago Tribune*, February 7, 1969.

88. Ibid.

89. Letter to Fred Taylor from Dr. Frank, July 20, 1964.

90. Letter from Dr. Frank to Frederick Schroeder.

91. From a letter written by Dr. Frank to the presidents of Taylor Wine, Pleasant Valley Wine Company, Gold Seal Vineyards and Hammondsport Wine Company, May 20, 1972.

92. Memo written by John P. Tomkins to colleagues in the Department of Pomology, Cornell University, January 11, 1973.

PART IV

93. Fournier, "Scientific Look at Vinifera in the East."

94. From interview with Kevin Zraly, August 2012.

95. Letter from Willy Frank to William S. Decker, Esq., February 1, 1966.

96. Interview with Margrit Frank, July 2010.

97. Ibid.; interview with Fred Frank, 2011.

98. Interview with Hudson Cattell, September 2011.

99. Ibid.

100. Interview with Fred Frank.

101. Interview with Eric Volz, July 2011.

102. Karen MacNeil, *The Wine Bible* (New York: Workman Publishing Company, 2001), 717.

103. *Grape Research News* 8, no. 3 (December 1997): 2, Table 2. New York Wine and Grape Foundation.

104. Ibid., 3.

105. Interview with Margit Frank, July 2011.

106. Letter to William Clifford from Willy Frank.

107. Interview with Eric Volz.

108. Interview with Margrit Frank, July 2011; information also contained in Ed Van Dyne, "Dr. Frank: A Retrospective," *American Wine Society Journal* (Fall 1985).

PART V

109. Ben Dobbin, draft for Associated Press article, dated October 1995.

110. Ibid.

111. Discussion with Mike Elliot, June 2011.
112. Interview with Eric Frey, July 2010.
113. Ibid.
114. Interview with Dr. Frank by Hudson Cattell.
115. Interview with Marc Veraguth, 2011.
116. Ibid.
117. From conversations with Barbara Frank Guior, 2012 and 2013.
118. Atlantic Seaboard Wine Association, "Monteith Wine Bowl Trophy," http://www.aswawines.org/AwardsMonteithBowl.aspx.

INDEX

About the Author

Tom Russ is a professor at the College of Southern Maryland and the author of six books. He spent his summers growing up in the Finger Lakes region of New York and owns a home in Hammondsport, New York. Wine and food have long been among his passionate interests. The growth of the *vinifera* wines and the local food movement in the Finger Lakes is a natural area of interest, and the story of Dr. Konstantin Frank was a logical extension of that interest.